Reading History

Reading History

MICHAEL BURGER

UNIVERSITY OF TORONTO PRESS
Toronto Buffalo London

ISBN 978-1-4875-0560-8 (cloth)   ISBN 978-1-4875-3238-3 (EPUB)
ISBN 978-1-4875-2387-9 (paper)   ISBN 978-1-4875-3237-6 (PDF)

Library and Archives Canada Cataloguing in Publication

Title: Reading history / Michael Burger.
Names: Burger, Michael, 1962– author.
Description: Includes bibliographical references and index.
Identifiers: Canadiana (print) 20210224665 | Canadiana (ebook) 20210224762 |
    ISBN 9781487523879 (paper) | ISBN 9781487505608 (cloth) | ISBN 9781487532383 (EPUB) |
    ISBN 9781487532376 (PDF)
Subjects: LCSH: History – Methodology. | LCSH: Reading.
Classification: LCC D16 .B87 2021 | DDC 907.2–dc23

We welcome comments and suggestions regarding any aspect of our publications – please feel free to contact us at news@utorontopress.com or visit us at utorontopress.com.

Every effort has been made to contact copyright holders; in the event of an error or omission, please notify the publisher.

We wish to acknowledge the land on which the University of Toronto Press operates. This land is the traditional territory of the Wendat, the Anishnaabeg, the Haudenosaunee, the Métis, and the Mississaugas of the Credit First Nation.

University of Toronto Press acknowledges the financial support of the Government of Canada and the Ontario Arts Council, an agency of the Government of Ontario, for its publishing activities.

For Kayla, Lincoln, and Truman

Contents

List of Figures, Table, and Map

Figures

Table

Map

Preface

History students spend a lot of time reading. They read primary sources. They read specialized articles and monographs. They sometimes read popular histories. And they read textbooks. Yet students are beginners. As beginners, they need to learn the differences among these different kinds of readings: their different natures, their different challenges, and the different expectations one needs to bring to them. My aim is practical: a *vade mecum* that will enable students to read better. For this reason, the book is short. Students should spend more time reading things other than this book. The aim of brevity means I have not attempted to cover all possible readings students may meet in a history course, either primary or secondary; to do so would have made the book too long. In particular, the chapter on material evidence provides only a taste. The temptation to add "just one more thing" pulls constantly.

The suggestions for further reading give some indication of my debts in writing this book. In common with textbook practice, citations in this book are slim – confined to direct quotations. There are, however, a number of people to thank. Aaron Cobb generously criticized a chapter and counselled on intellectual virtues while Kim Pyszka read and improved the subchapter on archaeological evidence. Miriam Davis even more generously read all of the chapters and also graciously guided me on sources for the Axe Man of New Orleans. Steve Gish and Tim Henderson kindly offered suggestions as to readings. Auburn University at Montgomery's interlibrary loan librarians gamely handled every request I made. Richard Alston answered questions about the papyrus discussed in this book. Nancy Dupree of the Alabama Department of Archives and History advised on early nineteenth-century palaeography; so did Steve Engerrand of the Georgia Archives; he also shared his great expertise on the nineteenth-century Georgia governors' archives and their history and other points of concern regarding the letter edited in chapter 2. Keith Krawczynski generously entertained my questions about illiterates and writing in early America. Jacques Fuqua advised me on the geography of Tokyo. Robin Fleming directed me to work on the Roman amphora in chapter 6. Mike Fitzsimmons suggested meanings for terminology in the *cahiers de doléances*. Will Fenn, Phill Johnson, and the Auburn University Library staff stepped in to solve some last-minute problems posed by Covid 19 shutdowns. I am very grateful to Natalie Fingerhut of the University of Toronto Press for persistently suggesting that a book like this is needed. I have always relied on the kindness of copyeditors: Jenn Harris saved me from many errors. Alex Grieve and Barb Porter of the Press much eased the production of this book. Similarly, I'm thankful for the help of the various minions, largely unknown to me, of the Press – including the Press's anonymous readers, who improved this book in various ways. Savannah Hollis enthusiastically served as a second eye on the proofs. Of course, I alone am responsible for any remaining shortcomings.

PART I: INTRODUCTION

chapter one

Introduction

It looked like a woman's breasts and neck. Or so the archaeologist thought. I am writing here of a small (a little more than 1½ inches wide at most) carving in mammoth ivory found at Dolni Věstonice, in what is today the Czech Republic (see figure 1.1).

It was made about 23,000 years ago, in a time known today as "prehistory" (in other words, human history before ca. 3000 BC, when written documents began to be produced). To the archaeologist, here was yet another artifact proving that prehistoric people worshipped primarily a great mother goddess. And there was more: the predominance of goddesses meant the dominance of women – or at least their equality with men in contrast with women's later subordination. Early human society was matriarchal, unlike later, and more familiar, patriarchy.

But look at that artifact again. Another archaeologist has pointed out a small hole that may well have been for a string or cord. She notes that when a replica is hung from such a string – perhaps as a pendant? – it hangs horizontally, looking like an erect penis with testicles (figure 1.2).

Or, I would add, like a hummingbird, an animal now extinct in Europe but for which fossils have been found in central Europe, dating as early as ca. 30,000 BC.

There are further complications. The artifact was one of a group of similar objects. Perhaps they were to be worn as beads on a necklace? In that case, perhaps the pieces hung vertically against the chest or neck (and so looked more neck-and-breast-like) rather than horizontally (see figure 1.3)? This has not, however, been established through experiment.

Moreover, on some of these other artifacts, the stick-like portion is close to a stub – suggesting a neck more than a phallus (see figure 1.3). Of course, could these objects not have been used as jewelry at all? Perhaps they were hung in a doorway or even from a tree (and so hung horizontally, looking more like male genitalia or hummingbirds)? No clear evidence points to the right answer.

Figure 1.1 Artifact from Dolni Věstonice. From J. Jelínek, *The Pictorial Encyclopedia of the Evolution of Man* (London: Hamlyn Publishing Group, 1975), 407.

There is better evidence for prehistoric goddess worship, but I fear it is not very good. A number of prehistoric sculptures are clearly of women: the "Venus of Willendorf" – also found in central Europe and perhaps 25,000 years old – is a famous example. But were these sculptures of goddesses? There is no compelling reason to think so. And even if prehistoric people worshipped goddesses more than male gods, does that mean women were dominant or at least equal to men? Perhaps not. Indeed, there are certainly historical cases of societies that revered goddesses yet were patriarchal. For instance, in the Greek city of Athens in the fifth century BC, named for its patron goddess Athena, women were by law subordinated to men in a deeply patriarchal society.

People often use the past – or at least their own version of it – for their own ends. Such has been the story of prehistoric matriarchy. When this theory was developed in the later nineteenth century, it was thought by most of its proponents to support modern patriarchy. The earliest human society, they argued, was matriarchal. In later societies – like those in which these scholars lived – men governed women, thus proving that patriarchy marked a later (read: "more advanced") society. It was only in the late twentieth and early twenty-first centuries that feminists in significant numbers flipped this line of argument. Those feminists – but by no means all feminists – argued that prehistoric matriarchy showed not that

Figure 1.2 Replica of artifact from Dolni Věstonice hung on a string. From Alice B. Kehoe, "No Possible, Probable Shadow of Doubt." *Antiquity* 65, 246 (1991): 129–31, fig. 2.

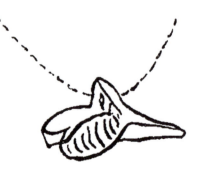
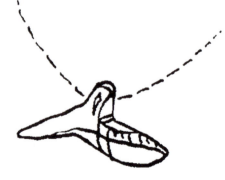

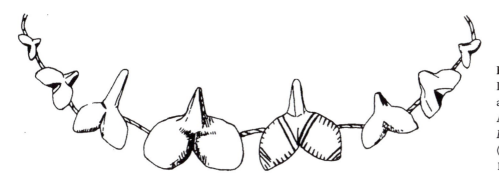

Figure 1.3 Artifacts from Dolni Věstonice imagined arranged as a necklace. From Alexander Marshak, *The Roots of Civilization*, rev. ed. (Mt. Kisco, NY: Moyer Bell, 1991), no. 223a.

men should rule women but that a society marked by full gender equality or even by female dominance was possible. Thus, such a society can, and should, exist again.

Both sides here used history. Or, to be more precise, they both abused it: creating a version of the past that never existed (or at least for which the evidence is weak) in order to advance their vision of how the world ought to be. And this point returns the discussion to that breasts-neck-penis-testicles-hummingbird artifact. The case for prehistoric matriarchy is only as strong as the evidence for it. As the contradictory readings of that artifact showed, however, it is all too easy to allow the conclusion one wants to get to – in this case, prehistoric matriarchy – to determine the conclusion one draws from evidence. When using historical evidence – or really any evidence – you should challenge the conclusions you draw from it, especially the conclusions you like. Not doing so can lead to serious error.

Indeed, it may be that the past never, by itself, really justifies a vision of the future. History is about what was. And what was, or even what is, does not in itself show what ought to be. "Ought" statements are statements of value. "Was" – or, for that matter, even "is" – statements are statements of fact, or at least that is the intent. Philosophers have spilled much ink writing about whether facts can ever by themselves show how things ought to be. I'll confine myself to observing that I have come across no compelling case that facts can do this. Indeed, the tale of prehistoric matriarchy I have recounted above illustrates the difficulty of getting from "was" to "ought." Both the patriarchally minded originators of the theory of prehistoric matriarchy and their feminist successors largely accepted the same picture of "was." But they came to contradictory conclusions about "ought."

My point about "was" not alone justifying "ought" does not mean, of course, that historians should not be inspired by their own times to ask new questions of the past. Any number of circumstances inspire historians – from a historian's religion, race, or politics to the time in which the historian lives, to sheer accidents of experience – the possibilities are endless. For example, the rise of feminism and the entry of many more women into the historical profession clearly help explain the rise of the history of women as a field in the last generation. But that does not mean that the conclusions reached by historians of women, no matter how well founded, can alone indicate what society ought to be like. Or indeed that any historian can achieve this.

So why bother doing history anyway? It has – at least – two uses. In the first place, understanding the past can help one better understand the present. Let me tell one short story to illustrate this. In the 1500s, Martin Luther, disagreeing with the medieval church on certain matters, started what became the Protestant Reformation. He did so not in the name of religious toleration, but in order that all Christians should, on their own, come to what he saw as the essential truths of the faith, truths the church of his own time, he believed, had obscured. But Christians failed to arrive at the agreement Luther expected; the result was religious war and massacre. By the end of the next century, some Western Christians were so appalled by the turmoil that they developed ideals of religious toleration. (I am simplifying here. For one thing, there were some other developments that also fostered the idea of religious tolerance, but I am keeping the story simple.) What this means is that modern Western thinking about religious freedom is not simply the product of some really smart people in the past suddenly understanding the right way to handle such matters. Instead, those ideals of religious freedom and tolerance were at least in part the product of people like Martin Luther, people who would have been appalled by them. And that understanding, in turn, can prompt you to consider for yourself whether those ideals are justified. In other words, understanding the past that produced your own world gives you a new perspective on it, one that prompts you to think about your world critically.

History's other use is more practical. Historians are detectives. Something happened in the past: the historian's job is to use what survives from the past as clues to reconstruct what happened both narrowly (what events took place? what were things like back then?) and more broadly (why did those events take place? why were things that way back then?). And what survives from the past to provide these clues? Primary sources. Most of this book is a guide to using different kinds of primary sources. No book can warn you about all the considerations that go into drawing conclusions from different primary sources. But this one aims to get you started by laying out some – although not all – of the different kinds of primary sources out there and some of the challenges they characteristically present. Historians mostly use written sources rather than what is sometimes called "material evidence," although historians have been giving such evidence more and more attention lately, which is still largely the province of archaeologists and art historians. (The artifact discussed previously is an example of such material evidence.) Like historians at large, this book will focus on written sources, although, as in this chapter, evidence that does not come in written form will get some attention too.

So why learn how to use primary sources? People make arguments based on evidence all the time. Politicians do it. Editorial writers do it. Lawyers in a court of law do it. Other people do it. And their arguments are often, unlike most scientific arguments, about non-repeating events – something that has happened only once. In other words, they are historical arguments. By learning how to draw conclusions from historical evidence yourself, you also learn how better to assess the arguments made by others. In other words, you develop a skill with consequences far beyond the classroom.

This point about evidence also goes to another problem that might seem to arise from the discussion of prehistoric matriarchy. That discussion may leave you thinking that primary sources do not matter because evidence does not really matter, that people inevitably draw whatever conclusions suit their agenda, their vision of what should be, regardless of the evidence. There is some truth to this, in the sense that people will always use (or abuse) evidence badly in just this way. But that does not mean that everyone does so. In particular, it does not mean that you have to. Some people are more careful than others. Some people are more self-disciplined than others. Some people are more honest than others. It's better to be careful, disciplined, and honest. I cannot, of course, prove this with historical evidence; it is an "ought" statement, after all. You will simply have to decide on other grounds whether you agree.

It is also worth noting that what inspires a historian to ask questions is different from the historian's responsibility to carefully and with discipline draw conclusions from evidence to answer those questions. While questions might come from beliefs about "ought," the answers are about "was." Indeed, traditionally, many historians have sought to avoid bias, like that evident in the debates over prehistoric matriarchy, bias that can often stem from beliefs about "ought." But bias can be the source of the inspiration, having a point of view that makes historical research happen. "Bias" gets its negative connotation from people refusing to allow evidence to correct their point of view. The key, then, is to collect evidence and read the evidence in a disciplined way even when – especially when – the evidence challenges your bias.

That point about being careful and disciplined points to another consideration that will be apparent from the next chapters. Using primary sources carefully is hard. Saying that historians' biases are such that people can never use sources well and so can never really know anything about the past anyway is easy. Taking that position can be simply an excuse to avoid the hard labor of working with evidence. But what happens to much of the rest of life if one takes the same approach? Think about those politicians, editorial writers, and lawyers, not to mention the detectives mentioned above. Is each of them just as correct as the rest? Or does evidence matter? The latter, I think.

A final matter. The conclusions historians draw from primary sources are found in secondary sources. Textbooks, more specialized books on history, scholarly articles in history journals – and your conclusions in papers and examinations – are all examples of secondary sources. This book will also give you some advice on reading secondary sources and alert you to some of the different kinds of secondary sources you may confront.

PART II: PRIMARY SOURCES

chapter two

From Manuscript to Edition

2.1 Editing

Most people first encounter written primary sources in books or, more recently, online. Most of those sources did not, however, start their lives between the covers of a book, much less on the internet. They started as manuscripts. Strictly speaking, a "manuscript" is something written by hand. A "typescript" is something that has been typed, as on a typewriter or, more recently, in a word-processing program. But historians often use the term "manuscript" loosely, to refer to both, so long as it has not yet been published. In that broad sense, it means something like "the original source that has not been typed (or retyped) *and* made available to the public in book or online form."

A lot of work goes into putting a primary source into your hands. This chapter aims to give you a greater appreciation of that fact – and to make you aware of the distance that still may remain between you, the reader curled up at home, and the primary source sitting in some lonely archive.

That lonely primary source may be handwritten, a true manuscript or "ms." The first job in making it available to readers traditionally is to produce a typed version of it – in other words, "transcribing" the text to produce a "transcript," indeed, a type-script.[1] More recently, an approach has been to scan (i.e., "digitize") or photograph the source and put the image online, but that will not be the case for most sources used by beginning history students. Transcription can be challenging. For one thing, hand-writing changes over time, producing new "scripts." Those changes can help one date a text (more on dating in what follows) but can also make handwriting hard to read for us moderns. Moreover, people who had to write a lot often made their work easier by

---

1 A transcript can also be a handwritten copy of the ms.

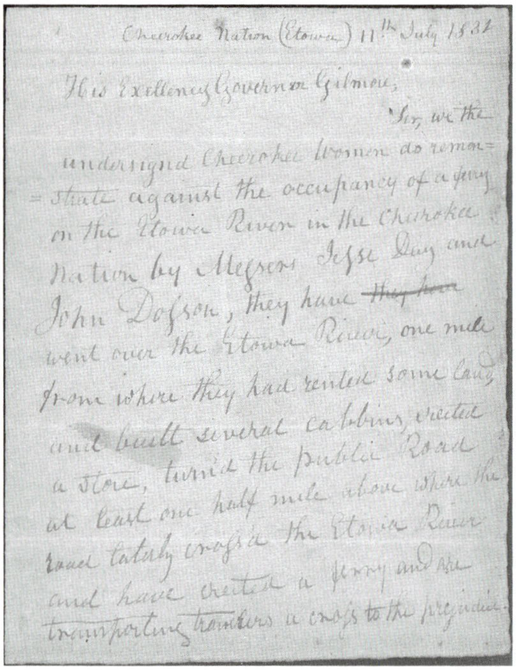

Figures 2.1 and 2.2 Letter to the governor of Georgia: front. Courtesy Georgia Archives, RG 4-2-46, File II Subjects, Indians – Cherokees, ah00874.

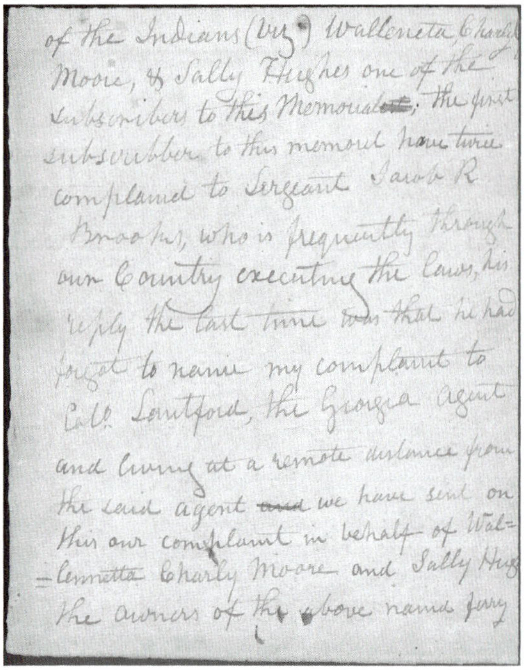

Figures 2.3 and 2.4 Letter to the governor of Georgia: back. Courtesy Georgia Archives, RG 4-2-46, File II Subjects, Indians – Cherokees, ah00874. https://vault.georgiaarchives.org/digital/collection/adhoc/id/1763/rec/91.

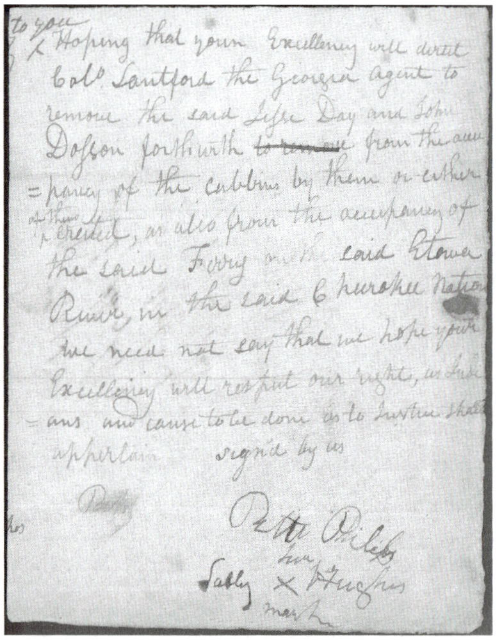

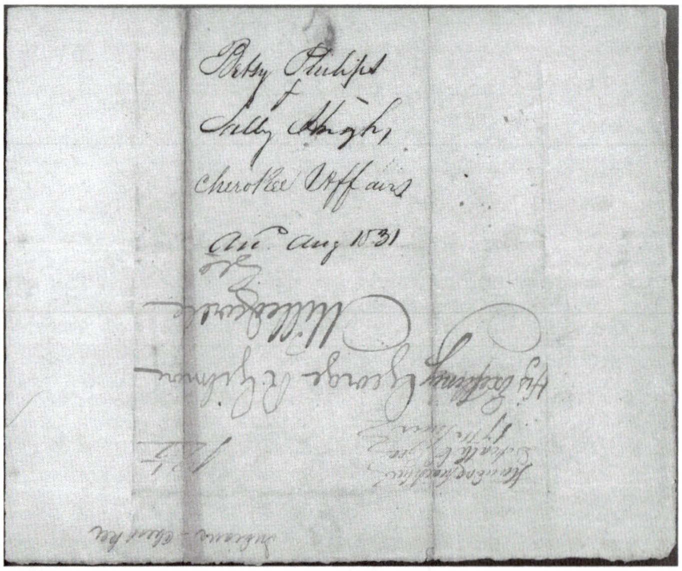

using a lot of abbreviations, some of which may no longer be used. So a person transcribing the source today needs to know what those abbreviations were and the various symbols that were sometimes used to make them. One modern guide to abbreviations used in medieval manuscripts has more than 13,000 entries.

Read the letter in figures 2.1–2.4, sent by two Cherokee women to the governor of Georgia in 1832.

If you found parts of the letter hard to read, you are not alone. Here is a transcript:

Cherokee Nation (Etowa) 11th July 1832
His Excellency Governor Gilmore,

Sir, we the undersigned Cherokee women do remonstrate against the occupancy of a ferry on the Etowa River in the Cherokee Nation by Messers Jesse Day and John Dosson, they have[2] went [sic] over the Etowa River, one mile from where they had rented some land, and built several cabbins [sic], erected a store, turn'd the public Road at least one half mile above where the road laterly [sic] cross'd the Etowa River and have erected a ferry and are transporting travelers a cross [sic] to the prejudice of the Indians (viz)[3] Walleneta, Charly Moore, and Sally Hughes one of the subscribers[4] to this Memorial;[5] the first subscribber [sic] to this memorial have [sic] twice complained to the Sergeant Jacob R Brooke, who is frequently through our country executing the laws, his reply the last time was that he had forgot to name my complaint to Colonel Santford, the Georgia agent and living at a remote distance from the said agent[6] we have sent this our complaint on behalf of the Wallennetta[7] Charly Moore and Sally Hughes the owners of the above named ferry to you[8][.] Hoping that your Excellency will direct Colonel Santford and the Georgia agent to remove the said Jesse Day and John Dosson forthwith[9] from the occupancy of the cabins by them or either of them[10] erected, as also from the occupancy of the said Ferry on the said Etowa River in the said Cherokee

"Sic," Latin for "thus," is used to indicate that yes, the ms really says that; the transcriber has not made an error. The square brackets [ ] are usually used, as here, to insert words or other matter into the text that are not in the original.

"Sic" here because the letter really does spell "cabins" with two "b"s.

---

2 "they have" is repeated, but crossed out.

3 An abbreviation for the Latin "videlicet," or "namely."

4 I.e., one of the people who signed below.

5 The ms reads "Memorialist" with the final "ist" crossed out.

6 "and" follows, but it is crossed out.

7 This word is spelled differently from its first occurrence.

8 "to you" inserted in the margin.

9 The words "to remove" follow but are crossed out.

10 "of them" inserted.

Nation we need not say that we hope your Excellency will respect our rights, as Indians and cause to be done as to Justice shall appertain[.] sign'd by us

Betsy Philips[11]
Her
Sally X Hughes
Mark

Note some of the issues that arise in transcription. For example, on the front (figure 2.1), the writer repeats the words "they have" and crosses them out again. Some transcriptions will give the reader a heads up about such corrections, perhaps with a footnote, as here. Other transcribers will choose not to do so. Note the abbreviation "Col°." for "Colonel"; a transcriber has to decide whether to extend (i.e., spell out) such words or leave them abbreviated, bearing in mind that abbreviations common in the past may be unknown today. Most such abbreviations will be extended in sources that you as a beginner will read. Another decision: should the transcriber transcribe the text as is or modernize it? For example, English speakers now write "turned," not "turn'd." This transcription keeps "turn'd," but another might modernize the text as "turned." Should misspellings (e.g., "cabbins" for "cabins") be corrected or not? The transcription can also require some careful observation. For example, letter forms sometimes need to be compared in order to figure out hard-to-read words. For example, the capital "E" of "Etowa" can be hard to identify as such the first time it appears, but comparing that letter form with "Etowa" three lines below clarifies that that first letter is indeed an "E." A modern reader might easily mistake the first "s" in the name "Dosson" for a "g" the first time that name appears. Again, later appearances of the name clarify that the letter is indeed an "s." One feature to note is two different forms of the letter "s" in one document; compare the first and second "s" in "cross'd" and "cross." This was at times a common practice, especially with the letter "s" when this letter was written.

Looking at the handwriting also raises a question: While Betsy Philips and Sally Hughes presumably composed this letter (that is, they decided what it would say), who actually put pen to paper? It is clear that Hughes did not do so, because rather than sign her name, she made her mark, a practice of the illiterate. But what about Philips? She did sign, so she could write. But her signature looks very different from the rest of the letter; indeed, it looks rather unpracticed. So, evidently, Philips and Hughes got someone else to put their words on paper, perhaps for a fee, perhaps as a favor. Could that person have also influenced what words were chosen? Perhaps.

There are some other physical aspects of the document to note. The letter as it now exists is in two sheets, each 6¾ by 8¼ inches. But it was originally a single sheet written in

---

11 "Betsy" appears to have been written to the left of this signature and then partly erased.

two columns. This is clear when you view the sheets next to each other, as photographed here. The "ges" of "Hughes" in the left column crosses the division between the two sheets, as do the brackets drawn in to keep the words "to you" inserted in the margin of the right column distinct from the left column. How to explain the fact of two sheets? The single sheet was apparently originally folded down the middle between the columns, a point that seems confirmed by the blob of orange wax (gray in this black-and-white photograph) to the far right, used to seal the letter closed in the days before envelopes.[12] Presumably natural decay turned the crease into an actual break, so one large sheet became two smaller ones; it is not clear why anyone would have deliberately cut the letter in two.

The back of the letter (figures 2.3 and 2.4) provides clues as to what happened to it after it was written. Three different people wrote on the back. There is the person who addressed the letter, noting that it was sent from Standing Peachtree, Dekalb County, GA (so, some distance from where the women operated their ferry), to the governor in Milledgeville, GA. The ink is in a shade close to that of the letter. A second hand, using darker ink, noted the letter was from Betsy Philips and Sally Hughes. That hand was probably that of someone in the governor's office, who also wrote the words "Indian Affairs," which gives a clue to how that office categorized the letter and filed it. Finally, a hand that has been identified as belonging to an archivist active in the Georgia Archives in the 1950s and 1960s added "Indians – Cherokee" in pencil, probably when the papers were organized by the state archives. The orange wax mentioned previously also appears at the top as a small gray blob in figure 2.2.

The study of handwritten letter forms is called "palaeography." Historians who specialize in early periods (before, say, ca. 1500) tend to receive specialized palaeographical training. This line from an English medieval (specifically thirteenth-century) bishop's register describes what this typically entailed (figure 2.5).

Like most documents from medieval Europe, it is written in Latin. I have extended the abbreviated bits with letters in square brackets [ ]. Read this transcription of the second line along with that line in the ms:

"Boyville ult[im]i r[e]ctor[is] eiusdem i[n] minorib[us] ordinib[us] p[re]sentat[us]."

And a last complication – the word in the line just above "presentatus": "ecc[lesi]am." (That very long horizontal stroke indicates the abbreviation.) Compare the two "c"s there in "ecclesiam" with the "t"s in "presentatus." As in many manuscripts in this period, they are virtually interchangeable. There is more to transcribing such

---

12 In an earlier period, wax seals typically bore the imprint of an image to authenticate the document, but by this time they were most often used simply to close up documents and bore no image.

The line over the "lti" indicates this is an abbreviation, hence the insertion of "im." A horizontal line over letters in this period often indicates that an "m" or "n" or a vowel followed by an "m" or "n" is to be inserted.

Note the abbreviation marks in the ms.

Note that the vertical downstrokes that make up the "i" and the "u" are close to indistinguishable. Such downstrokes are known as "minims," and were used in the thirteenth century to make the following letters: i, n, m, u; this can make the letters "mi" hard to distinguish from "im" or "uu" or "iui." Here a faint horizontal stroke floats over the "iu." It really belongs with the "i," and is the medieval equivalent of our dot over the "i." Not all scribes even bothered with that stroke.

Now perhaps you can recognize the horizontal stroke indicating, in this case, an "n" is to be inserted.

Have fun with these minims!

What looks like a "3" is an abbreviation mark, usually for "us."

This kind of squiggle after a "p" typically means one should read "pre," "prae," or "pro."

This squiggle, especially at the end of a word, indicates "us." When better formed, there is a hole in the thickest part, and so it looks more like a circle with a tail. Like letters, sometimes abbreviation marks are not well formed.

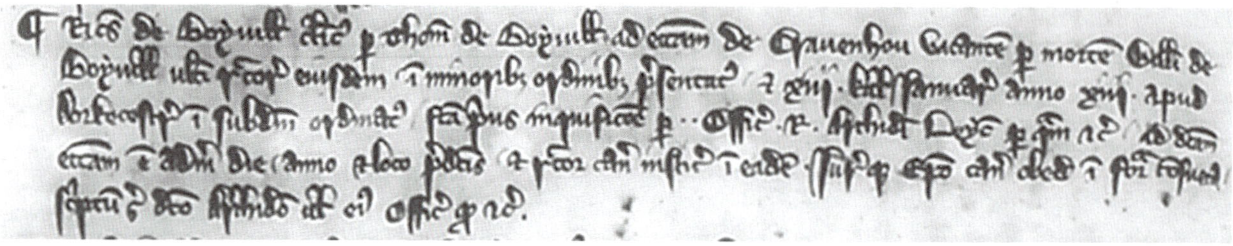

Figure 2.5 F. 283 v, first two lines of second entry. Lincolnshire Archives Office [UK], Episcopal Register I f. 283 v.

manuscripts than memorizing abbreviation marks. It requires experience reading such texts and so simply recognizing words, words like "ecclesiam." It should also at this point be obvious that letter forms change over time. Compare, for example, the "s" in "eiusdem" in the first line of the medieval script with either form of "s" in "cross'd" in the letter of 1832. Indeed, a manuscript's script itself can help to date it.

And transcription can be the easy part. Consider that much discussed work of ancient Greek literature, the *Odyssey* by Homer: a tale of the adventures of Odysseus, a Greek king and veteran of the Trojan War, in his ten-year quest to return home after the war's end.

One of the first things one wants to know about a primary source is when it was written. Sometimes the source itself very conveniently indicates its date, as in the above letter: July 11, 1832. The *Odyssey*, however, does not. Pick up almost any modern copy of the *Odyssey* and you will read that it was written ca. 800–700 BC. How do modern scholars know this? Produced in a world before the printing press, like most written works, the *Odyssey* survived by being copied and copied and copied again. And modern readers were lucky that the *Odyssey* was so popular and copied so much; otherwise, it may not have survived. But the earliest complete surviving copy of the *Odyssey* dates to the tenth or eleventh centuries. Other evidence, however, allows one to date the work much earlier. Greek works from the seventh century BC on frequently refer to the *Odyssey*, often quoting a line or two. Those quotations are the same or very close to that tenth/eleventh-century manuscript, moving the work's date much earlier. Could the work date much, much earlier? Ancient Greeks thought Homer wrote two works, the *Odyssey* and the *Iliad*, which concerned the Trojan War itself, in which the Greeks, led by the king of Mycenae, one of several Greek kings, besieged Troy. In the later nineteenth century, the archaeologist Heinrich Schliemann excavated what appeared to be the long-lost city of ancient Troy and followed up by finding the site of ancient Mycenae. Since the ancient Greeks themselves traditionally dated the Trojan War to ca. 1200 BC, and Schliemann's sites seemed also to date to about this time, perhaps that was when the poems were composed – or at least, that was the time of the society the poems depicted. Schliemann died believing this.

But matters are not so simple. There are big discrepancies between the world depicted in the *Odyssey* – and that in the *Iliad* – and the society Schliemann dug up.

Documents written in a script called Linear B found at Mycenae were written in Greek, so at least we know that that society spoke Greek like its later inhabitants. But those documents – mostly bookkeeping concerning the king's possessions – show kings even richer than the ones in Homer. In the *Odyssey*, Odysseus's swineherd could know from memory how much livestock Odysseus had – no need for the elaborate record keeping of the Linear B tablets. Although the *Odyssey*'s author takes great pains to stress the magnificence of Odysseus's palace, it doesn't match the glories of Mycenaean-age rulers. A detail in the *Odyssey* gives the game away: Odysseus's palace turns out to have a dirt floor. Odysseus himself is not that far removed from the farmers who would have been far below the kings of the Mycenaean age; he knows how to plough a furrow straight and built his bed himself. The great in Mycenae were interred in impressive tombs; Homer's dead are cremated. And so on. Thus, ca. 1200 BC is not right for the *Odyssey*.

Why ca. 800–700 BC? Because the society depicted in the *Odyssey* – and the *Iliad* – seems a better "fit" for a later period. The collapse of Mycenaean civilization ca. 1100 BC was followed by a long period, the Greek Dark Ages (ca. 1100–800 BC). Linear B, indeed any form of writing, disappeared, along with archaeological evidence of large settlements, big palaces, and trade. "Homer" – modern historians are not persuaded he really existed and are not even certain whether the same person actually composed the *Iliad* and the *Odyssey* – seems to be depicting a much less economically developed society in which "kings" were simply great aristocrats. Greek society as it appears ca. 800 BC and a bit later looks very much like an aristocratically dominated society with kings scarcely to be found. Homer's works themselves appear to have been composed orally and handed down by word of mouth over one or more generations. This circumstance would explain, among other things, why about a third of the poems are repeated word for word elsewhere in the same poem: such repetition made memorization easier. Another sign of an oral society is that the poems never refer to writing. So while someone composed the *Odyssey* verbally, it eventually was written down. The composition should precede the widespread reintroduction of writing into Greece – so, by 700 BC. (Even then, there are problems. For one thing, the metal most often mentioned in the *Odyssey*, and in the *Iliad*, is bronze, yet the Greeks widely used iron in the Greek Dark Ages and after.)

So, a tortuous business – only barely explored here – lies behind the simple line "the *Odyssey*, ca. 800–700 BC" in modern translations of the work. Not every source requires this much detective work when it comes to dating. But many do.

As to where the *Odyssey* was composed: since the source is in Greek and about Greeks, presumably it was composed in the Greek-speaking world – so, in what is today modern Greece or the western coast of modern Turkey. Homer's Greek is mostly the version of ancient Greek known as "Ionian," which narrows the location to the Greek islands of the Ionian Sea and Turkey's western coast.

So there are answers to "when?" and "where?" it was written. But there is the matter of the text itself. As noted, the oldest complete copy dates from many, many years after the poem was written down. It is the result of the *Odyssey* being frequently copied – indeed, scraps of some of those earlier copies have been recovered from the dry, preserving sands of ancient Egyptian garbage dumps. As a text is copied, and copied again from copies, errors occur. Think of a game of "telephone," in which a message is passed from person to person; the last person receives a message almost always different in some way from the original. This process can lead to many, many surviving copies, all with slight (or even major) variations. Carefully comparing these copies allows scholars to reconstruct which were copies from which, often with the hypothesis of lost copies that came between surviving ones in the chain. The result is what is called a "stemma" (Greek for "wreath" – think of twigs twisted together), a kind of family tree of manuscripts. And that work in turn helps scholars establish a correct text – that is, the closest version to the lost original. Indeed, ancient Greeks were already working on establishing a correct text of Homer's work from various copies in the third century BC. So, just getting the text that you are reading right may have been a major endeavor.

2.2 Kinds of Editions: Print and Online

All this labor results in an edition of the source, by which it is made available to the larger public. You might find an edition between the covers of a book or you might find it on the World Wide Web. In either case, editions come in various forms.

A scholarly edition is one that comes with a fairly extensive analysis of the text, not in order to draw grand historical conclusions – that's primarily the reader's job – but in order to give the reader the fullest understanding of the text. This discussion will likely include the various arguments needed to establish the date and provenance of the source, not to mention what can be uncovered about how the text was produced. It may well have extensive notes explaining characteristics of the text (such as holes in the paper or abbreviations) or explaining the text's special terms or other features that even specialists might not know. Such editions are typically prepared for professionals and more advanced students, but they can be revealing for the dedicated beginner. They are most often found in book form, but they can appear online too. Consider, for example, the edition of the American Declaration of Independence, to be found online in the *Papers of Thomas Jefferson*.[13]

---

13 https://jeffersonpapers.princeton.edu/selected-documents/declaration-independence, accessed July 29, 2020.

If you go to that website, notice that it includes an "editorial note" that not only points to what scholars have said about the stages in which the Declaration was drafted but also includes its own analysis of those stages. Even better, a "related documents" section provides the surviving texts of the Declaration or documents that led to the final version, what this website describes as "The Declaration of Independence as Adopted by Congress."[14] Looking at that version and scrolling to the end (after the signatures) provides more information about early copies of the final version:

> Engrossed and signed parchment copy (DNA) as engraved by W. J. Stone in 1823 and reproduced in Force, *Archives*, 5th ser., I, facing col. 1597-8. Among the three official texts of the Declaration of Independence, the parchment copy, believed to have been engrossed by Timothy Matlack (DAB, art. on Matlack) and known to have been signed on 2 Aug. 1776 (JCC, v, 626), generally takes precedence. On the signing, see Editorial Note to TJ's Notes of Proceedings in the Continental Congress, 7 June to 1 Aug. 1776. Respecting the capitalization and punctuation of this text, see a comment by Carl Becker, quoted at the end of the general Editorial Note, above. The parchment copy was, by law, in the custody of the Department of State from 1789. In 1823 a lithographed facsimile in an edition of 200 copies was made by W. J. Stone, and the copies were distributed in accordance with a joint resolution of Congress of 26 May 1824. (As a surviving signer, TJ received two copies; see Secretary of State J. Q. Adams to TJ, 24 June 1824, and TJ's acknowledgment of 18 July 1824.) From 1841 to 1877 the parchment copy was exhibited in the Patent Office, and from then until 1894 in the Department of State. In the latter year, because the text had been seriously damaged both by the wet-press process Stone had used in making his facsimile and by many years' exposure to light (see photograph in Michael, cited below, between p. 14–15), it was put away in a steel case in the Department, and a facsimile was exhibited instead. By executive order in 1921 the custody of the engrossed and signed copies of both the Declaration and the Constitution was transferred to the Librarian of Congress, and on 28 Feb. 1924 these two documents were placed in a bronze and marble shrine on the second floor of the Library, where they remain on perpetual exhibit under proper guard. (William H. Michael, *The Declaration of Independence: Illustrated Story of Its Adoption*, Washington, 1904; Hazelton, *Declaration of Independence*, ch. IX and notes; Gaillard Hunt, *The Department of*

---

14 "The Declaration of Independence as Adopted by Congress," *The Papers of Thomas Jefferson*, accessed July 29, 2020, https://jeffersonpapers.princeton.edu/selected-documents/declaration-independence-adopted-congress.

State of the United States, New Haven, 1914, p. 295–313; Librarian of Congress, *Annual Report for 1949*, p. 36ff.)[15]

You should note that the material on this website was first edited in book form: *The Papers of Thomas Jefferson I: 1760–1776*, eds. Julian P. Boyd et al. (Princeton: Princeton University Press, 1950), 413–33. As stated earlier, most scholarly editions – in fact, most editions period – appear in book form. And most editions on the internet are, like this one, web versions of what had originally been published old school, in print. You may also note that this press is a "university press": a publisher in theory subsidized by a university in order to publish books of scholarly value that are not likely to sell well and so not likely to find a commercial publisher. Scholarly editions are most often, although not always, published by university presses; most that are not are published by presses that specialize in publishing books for scholars (sometimes called "academic presses") – typically very expensive books, mostly destined for deep-pocketed university libraries.

But there are more popular editions too. Consider the appearance of the Declaration of Independence on CNN's website.[16] The CNN webpage produces the Declaration's text and just the text: no commentary, no explanatory notes. It does not attempt the kind of reconstruction evident in the Princeton.edu edition previously discussed.

The CNN edition is useful – the text appears without commentary, but the text is correct. Other editions are less useful. An example is on the website "Owlcation.org." Here is its presentation of the Declaration's first sentence:

> *When in the Course of human events, it becomes necessary for one people to dissolve the political bands which have connected them with another, and to assume among the powers of the earth, the separate and equal station to which the Laws of Nature and of Nature's God entitle them, a decent respect to the opinions of mankind requires that they should declare the causes which impel them to the separation.*

The Declaration of Independence begins with what is commonly referred to [as] the Introduction. Although it's actually just one, albeit long, sentence with a simple meaning, there's a lot we can take from it.

---

15 "The Declaration of Independence as Adopted by Congress," *The Papers of Thomas Jefferson*, accessed July 29, 2020, https://jeffersonpapers.princeton.edu/selected-documents/declaration-independence-adopted-congress.

16 "Read the Full Text of the Declaration of Independence," CNN, accessed July 29, 2020, https://www.cnn.com/2019/07/04/us/declaration-of-independence-full-text-trnd/index.html.

At a general level, the Introduction simply states why the document is even being written. The Founders thought that, out of respect, they should tell their former government, Great Britain, why they feel the need to leave.

Looking at the details, we see at first very elegant writing. From this, we take away that the Founders were very educated, and they were. They were all scholars of some field, and had vast knowledge, both about their present (and our present) and the past, on various topics, including politics. This elegant writing doesn't go away, not in this document, or the Constitution, or the Federalist Papers. In fact, it stays around even into the Civil War, where it's seen in the Gettysburg Address....[17]

Notice that this edition of the Declaration has a lot of commentary, but the commentary is addressed to relatively inexperienced readers – it points out, for example, that the first sentence is very long and that it, being an introduction, announces the document's purpose. As a student, you should probably avoid such websites, as the point of reading primary sources is to figure out what they mean yourself. This approach is taken even further by the following, seen in another online edition, which attempts to "translate" the Declaration into a simpler and more modern English style (the "translations" appear here in italics):

When in the Course of human events, it becomes necessary for one people to dissolve the political bands which have connected them with another, and to assume among the powers of the earth, the separate and equal station to which the Laws of Nature and of Nature's God entitle them, a decent respect to the opinions of mankind requires that they should declare the causes which impel them to the separation.

When it becomes necessary to end one political process due to lack of representation, it's only fair to list the reasons why.

We hold these truths to be self-evident, that all men are created equal, that they are endowed by their Creator with certain unalienable Rights, that among these are Life, Liberty and the pursuit of Happiness.--

We believe everyone is created equal, and should be afforded the right to pursue life, liberty, and happiness as they see it. We believe these rights a fundamental truth, and no government's right to curtail, now, and forever more....[18]

---

17 Jason, "Analysis of the Declaration of Independence," Owlcation, accessed July 29, 2020, https://owlcation .com/social-sciences/Analysis-of-the-Declaration-of-Independence.

18 "The Declaration of Independence – modern translation 2012," GoogleDocs, accessed July 29, 2020, https://docs. google.com/document/d/17-kk6FR8PGku4XhCy2TFBSbEeIWUlm082qgaqXAP81Y/mobilebasic?pli=1.

If you scroll to the end of this webpage, you will find some commentary that goes far beyond the document itself, embracing current political values and reading the Declaration in that light:

> As is mentioned in the video "Don't be a Sucker" on YouTube, we're a nation of minorities. Whenever we let anyone impinge on someone else's rights, it's only a matter of time before we lose our own.
>
> "Together we stand" doesn't mean we stand together against this or that group, it means we're all strong by supporting other people's values. Difference is what makes each of us and this country strong. Respect the choices others make, it's the American Way.[19]

Whether or not you agree with the point of view expressed here, the fact is that the webpage is attempting to use the source to prove a point about current issues. That should make you hesitate about relying on this commentary or, indeed, the "translation." Remember the discussion of "was" statements and "ought" statements in chapter 1: here the editor's commitment regarding "ought" may very well shade the editor's rendering of "was."

The kind of edition beginning history students are most likely to encounter is a primary source anthology, often called a "reader." Such collections are put together with students in mind. The goal is to offer each source with an introduction that provides some basic information for initially making sense of the source without doing students' work for them. The source will likely also have footnotes or endnotes to explain things in the source that a beginner would need, so you will probably find notes for terms that go unexplained in a scholarly edition, which is produced for readers who already have a good knowledge of the field, if not that particular source. A good example of this kind of edition is the Roman property deed discussed in chapter 3 – notice all the footnotes.

The aforementioned webpages also present some lessons about reading primary sources online. Webpages operated by universities are especially likely to present scholarly and reliable editions, such as the Princeton University website here. Government websites tend to be good in this way too – so, look for .edu or .gov.

The Owlcation.com website, in contrast, describes itself as a website produced by "a diverse group of engineers, product and community advocates, moderators, and editors that are passionate about writing and online know-how. In addition to our official team, we are a tight-knit community of thousands of writers and enthusiasts."[20] In other

---

19 Ibid.

20 https://owlcation.com/about-us, accessed October 29, 2020.

words, the people editing the primary sources that appear on the site may have historical expertise, but one cannot count on it. The upside of this approach is that Owlcation can offer webpages on a huge variety of subjects: from identifying caterpillars to Emily Dickinson to, yes, the Declaration of Independence. This lack of expertise probably also applies to the CNN website. And both have a particular need to gain clicks, which may make them less choosy about the quality of the material posted; notice the advertisements on those webpages, which are absent from Princeton.edu. The last webpage discussed above, with the "translation" of the Declaration, appears in Google Docs with no further indication of affiliation – not a promising sign. Remember that anyone can put anything up on the web. Publishers of books, on the other hand, typically have a more extensive process for vetting what they publish; academic and university presses tend to be especially careful, although their controls can go wrong too.

2.3 Translations

Of course, if the source is in a language you cannot read, it has to be translated. Such translation is a kind of veil between you and the source itself, albeit a necessary one if you do not read the original language. Consider these translations of the first lines of the *Odyssey* – look for commonalities and differences:

Translation of Samuel Butler:[21]

> Tell me, O muse, of that ingenious hero who travelled far and wide after he had sacked the famous town of Troy. Many cities did he visit, and many were the nations with whose manners and customs he was acquainted; moreover he suffered much by sea while trying to save his own life and bring his men safely home; but do what he might he could not save his men, for they perished through their own sheer folly in eating the cattle of the Sun-god Hyperion; so the god prevented them from ever reaching home. Tell me, too, about all these things, O daughter of Jove, from whatsoever source you may know them.

Translation of Robert Fagles:[22]

> Sing to me of the man, Muse, the man of twists and turns
> driven time and again off course, once he had plundered

---

21 Homer, *The Odyssey*, trans. Samuel Butler (London: A.A. Littlefield, 1900), 1.

22 Homer, *The Odyssey*, trans. Robert Fagles (New York: Penguin, 1996), 77.

the hallowed heights of Troy.

Many cities of men he saw and learned their minds,

many pains he suffered, heartsick on the open sea,

fighting to save his life and bring his comrades home.

But he could not save them from disaster, hard as he strove –

the recklessness of their own ways destroyed them all,

the blind fools, they devoured the cattle of the Sun

and the Sungod wiped from sight the day of their return.

Launch out on his story, Muse, daughter of Zeus,

start from where you will – sing for our time too.

Translation of Stanley Lombardo:[23]

Speak, Memory –

        Of the cunning hero,

The wanderer, blown off course time and again

After he plundered Troy's sacred heights.

        Speak

Of all the cities he saw, the minds he grasped,

The suffering deep in his heart at sea

As he struggled to survive and bring his men home

But he could not save them, hard as he tried –

The fools – destroyed by their own recklessness,

When they ate the oxen of Hyperion the Sun,

And that god snuffed out the day of their return.

        Of these things,

Speak, Immortal One,

And tell the tale once more in our own time.

Arguably, these translators have Homer saying much the same thing: that this will be the story of Odysseus, who traveled to many places before he reached home, that he tried to save his men but failed because his men foolishly ate the sun god's cattle.

But there are differences. Most obviously, Butler's translation is in prose, whereas Fagles and Lombardo both write in verse. Fagles's and Lombardo's decision makes sense, as the original is also in verse, and so in that way they are producing something closer to the original text. But verse imposes limits in terms of meter or rhyme or both – prose translations are thus usually more literal than verse translations. Usually, but

---

23 Homer, *Odyssey*, trans. Stanley Lombardo (Indianapolis: Hackett, 2000), 1.

not necessarily. Take Butler's description of Odysseus as "ingenious." This does get at an important characteristic of Odysseus. But Homer's Greek here says that Odysseus is characterized by "polutropos," "many turnings." In other words, he is not just ingenious in the sense of being inventive, but he is, as Lombardo puts it, "cunning," or, better, as Fagles translates, a man of "twists and turns." Odysseus is tricky. This is, after all, the character in legend who came up with the Trojan Horse. There is also a kind of pun here, as Odysseus's journey home also takes many twists and turns.

Even leaving aside the Greek, one can see different choices made by the translators. Butler and Lombardo, for example, both tell readers the name of the sun god whose cattle Odysseus's men foolishly ate: Hyperion. A reader of Lombardo might be a little unclear on whom the poet is addressing: "memory." The other translations are more explicit, making clear that the person addressed is a muse (a kind of goddess) and indeed the daughter of Zeus, the chief god. (Although Butler has the annoying habit of using the Roman names for Greek gods, so Zeus appears here as "Jove.") Lombardo does near the end tell readers that memory is immortal, which might suggest a god or goddess, but that's about it. (That memory here is some kind of person, and an important one, is indicated by Lombardo by capital letters in **bold**, a feature that does not appear in the Greek.) And did Odysseus on his travels visit *many* cities (Butler and Fagles) or just cities (Lombardo)? All agree that Odysseus looted Troy, but Troy itself is revered in Fagles and Lombardo ("hallowed," "sacred") but simply "famous" in Butler.

Most beginning students can, for practical purposes, ignore the translation problem. But you should be aware that it exists, and it explains why the professionals almost always use sources in their original language.

Transcription, establishment of a correct text (if need be), establishment of date and place of composition, and (if need be) translation: all of these elements go into creating the version of the source that most of us read, the edition. The person responsible for the edition, which may also include a helpful introduction and notes (footnotes at the bottom of the page or endnotes at the back) explaining the text, is the "editor," or, if a translation, sometimes also the translator. You should thank yours.

chapter three

Primary Source Basics and Two Documents of Practice

When you approach a primary source, there are a lot of questions to answer. Answering them often requires reading the source more than once; each pass allows you to deal with higher-order issues or even just increase your understanding of the source or notice what you missed before. While the following chapters will address questions that pertain to different kinds of primary sources, here I will (mostly) focus on the questions you can ask of any primary source.

3.1 Questions about the Source

Your first job is to establish some basic facts about the source. You should do this even before worrying about drawing historical conclusions from it. Be aware that the editor's introduction and notes may well answer some of these questions. Be sure you know the answers – insofar as you can know them – before trying to draw other conclusions about the source.

- **Who, what, where, when?** *Who produced the source? What kind of source is it? (E.g., a personal letter? A law?) When was it produced? Where was it produced?* If there is an editor's introduction to the source, it will likely answer some or all of these questions.
- **Audience?** *Who seems to have been the expected audience?* This may be easy to figure out. It may be impossible to do so. But most people tailor what they say toward their target audience. People in the past did too. If your source's expected audience shaped what it says, that can affect the conclusions you can draw from it.
- **Preservation?** *How was the source preserved? Who would have preserved it, and why?* You might well not be able to answer these questions. You're more likely to find the answer in the editor's introduction rather than the source itself. Sometimes the answer

is important. If generations between the creation of the source and the present deliberately took steps to preserve it, these people acted as a kind of filter, making some sources more likely to survive and, by implication, some less likely to do so. And that fact, in turn, might result in the surviving source misleading readers about the past.

- **Literacy?** *How important is it that the source was produced – in other words, written – in the first place?* Throughout most of human existence, most people were illiterate. If most people in a society were illiterate, documents from that society may represent the views of only a small portion of the population, often the elite. That said, in some times and places, the illiterate hired the literate to produce the documents they needed. In such situations, a third party still mediates between the illiterate person and the document you are reading. (Consider the letter sent by Betsy Philips and Sally Hughes in chapter 2.) These factors may have an impact on the conclusions you draw from the document.

- **Meaning?** *Is the source trying to say or show something?* If so, in your own words, explain what. Your mission here is to establish what the source is saying. At this point, do not worry about whether the source's claims are right or wrong or what historical conclusions you can draw from it. Try to be sympathetic to the author, even if you hate what the author says. (Indeed, especially if you hate what the author says.) Answering this question will often be the hardest thing you have done so far. In the case of a source that presents an elaborate and difficult argument, it can be very hard. But you will not be in a good position to use the source as historical evidence if you do not understand what it says.

Now let's see how these questions can illuminate an actual source. This one is short, so, unlike most sources in this book, it's reproduced here in its entirety. My comments are in the "balloons" in the margins.

A man buys a house in Roman Egypt

The dry sands of Egypt have preserved many papyri, i.e., pieces of papyrus paper, rarely complete, which people in Egypt either lost or threw away over the centuries. Thousands of such papyri dating from the time of Roman rule have been recovered from Oxyrhynchus, which served as the capital of the Oxyrhynchite nome, one of the roughly thirty territorial divisions – or nomes – of Egypt; these nomes dated back to before Egypt's conquest by Alexander the Great in the fourth century B.C. The writing on most of the papyri, including this one, is in Greek. In A.D. 55, when this document was produced, Egypt was under Roman rule.

Marginal notes (left column):

Editors sometimes invent titles for sources, especially when the source appears in a collection or reader. Be wary of drawing conclusions from such invented titles – but they can be helpful.

This section, here in *italics*, is by the editor. What follows is the primary source itself. Unless noted otherwise, notes will typically be the editor's.

Preservation? This information helps answer the matter of how the document was preserved. Someone threw it away or lost it. So, presumably, the document at some point was no longer important enough to keep. The Egyptian sands did the rest. In other words, this source survives almost entirely as a result of chance rather than because people had a motive to preserve it for centuries.

Where? The editor's introduction tells you where the document comes from: Oxyrhynchus in Egypt. That takes care of "Where?"

Audience? The editor does not say much about an intended audience. But at least one can say the expected reader read Greek.

Who? and **Literacy?** As to who wrote it: the fact that it was written in Greek opens the door to the possibility that Tryphon (who, as will be seen below, appears to have identified as Greek) wrote it. Or perhaps, this being a legal document, he did what people today normally do: hire someone with legal expertise to write it. The document itself does not say who composed it. Certainly Tryphon had the biggest interest in having the document produced: it proves his title to his house!

The second year of Nero Claudius Caesar Augustus Germanicus[1] Imperator, on the 6th of the month Audnaeus[2]=Sebastus,[3] at Oxyrhynchus in the Thebaid,[4] before the agoranomi[5] Andromachus and Diogenes.[6] Tryphon, son of Dionysius,[7] about …[8] years old, of middle height, fair, with a long face and a slight squint, and having a scar on his right wrist, has bought from his mother Thamounis's cousin, Pnepheros, son of Papontos,[9] also an inhabitant of Oxyrhynchus, about 65 years old, of middle height, fair, having a long face and a scar above his …[10] eyebrow and another on his right knee, (the document being drawn up in the street) one half of a three-storied house inherited from his mother, together with all its entrances and exits and appurtenances, situated by the Serapeum[11] at Oxyrhynchus in the southern part of the street called Temgenouthis to the west of the lane leading to "Shepherds' Street," its boundaries being, on the south and east, public roads, on the north, the house of the aforesaid Thamounis, mother of Tryphon the buyer, on the west, the house of Tausiris, sister of Pnepheros the seller, separated by a blind alley, for the sum of 32 talents[12] of copper; and Pnepheros undertakes to guarantee the half share which is sold perpetually in every respect with every guarantee.

When? Here the document, along with the footnotes, adds a little detail as to "when": roughly November.

What? This pretty well summarizes the document. It records in a formal way the purchase of a house by Tryphon from Pnepheros. The document is what we might call a "bill of sale" or perhaps a "title deed."

Audience? Since it's a bill of sale, it was also presumably meant to be produced in a court of law and may therefore aim to allay a later dispute about ownership of the house.

Where? Even greater detail as to where. Most sources are not nearly this specific! Count yourself lucky.

So what answers emerge to the aforementioned questions? The document was produced in the year 55, in about November, in Oxyrhynchus, in Egypt. It's a bill of sale for a house, sold by Pnepheros, son of Papontos to Tryphon, son of Dionysius. Being a bill of sale, it was presumably intended to be read by a court of law should the sale or title ever be disputed: that would be the expected audience. Indeed, these observations also basically answer the question of what the document seems to be trying to say: that Pnepheros sold a house to Tryphon in Oxyrhynchus, with some additional detail as to where it's located, identifying details as to the buyer and seller, the purchase price (32 talents of copper); it also says that Pnepheros guarantees the sale. As to why this source

---

1 Better known as the Roman emperor Nero.

2 A Macedonian month, roughly November.

3 Another term, of Roman origin, for the same month.

4 The nomes of Egypt were grouped into three large districts, of which the Thebaid was the southernmost.

5 Market regulators; one of the chief officials of the nome's capital town.

6 Both Greek names.

7 Both Greek names.

8 Word(s) missing.

9 All three Egyptian names.

10 Portion missing.

11 A temple of Sarapis, a god created under the Pharaoh Ptolemy I out of aspects of Greek and Egyptian gods.

12 A unit of currency. Talents could also come in gold or silver.

survives: sheer chance, given how papyri have come down to the present. One should not conclude that the fact the source survives is rooted in some kind of bias.

3.2 Drawing Historical Conclusions: Questions about the World beyond the Source

Always remember that your answers to the previous questions are only a step toward the larger goal of most historians, who are usually concerned not only with the source, but also with the world that produced the source, the world that lay behind the source. The following questions are hardly exhaustive, as you will see.

- **Conclusions about time and place?** *What conclusions can you draw from the source about the time and place that produced it?*
- **Limits imposed by time and place?** *Do your answers to the prior set of questions – about who produced the source, etc. – in any way influence or limit what conclusions you can draw?*

There are also narrower questions that might help you draw historical conclusions from the source; in other words, help you answer the above questions. Here is a (far from exhaustive) list. Not all of them will pertain to every source. Many of them will likewise come up again – with greater detail – in subsequent chapters on different kinds of sources.

- **Actions?** *Does the source provide evidence of actions taken by people in the past? If so, what conclusions can you draw from those actions? How well informed can you suppose the writer to have been about the events recounted? How reliable a reporter?*
- **Authority?** *What or whom does the source seem to view as authoritative?* This can tell you something about what was revered at the time. A source that, for example, cites the Canadian Parliament or the Bible indicates that the writer at least expects his or her audience to respect the Parliament or the Bible.
- **Groups?** *Does the source divide people into groups in any way? If so, what are those groups? Does the source make assumptions about how those groups or members of them do or should relate to one another?* Here, you may note clues as to how the source expects society to be structured – or at least how the writer thought it should be structured.
- **Relationships?** *What kinds of connections between people can you identify? What connects people?* Your answers may well be related to those of the previous question.

- **Good and bad?** *Does the source make moral distinctions? If so, what is viewed as good? As bad? What values does the source seem to assume?*
- **Argument?** *If the source makes an argument, what is it? What issues seem to be debated in this society?*
- **Explain?** *Does the source attempt to explain anything? If so, how does it go about doing so?*
- **Assumptions?** *What knowledge or conditions does the source take for granted?* This can serve as evidence of what was expected in the time and place that produced the source.

Now reread the source with these new questions in mind.

A man buys a house in Roman Egypt

The dry sands of Egypt have preserved many papyri, i.e., pieces of papyrus paper, rarely complete, which people in Egypt either lost or threw away over the centuries. Thousands of such papyri dating from the time of Roman rule have been recovered from Oxyrhynchus, which served as the capital of the Oxyrhynchite nome, one of the roughly thirty territorial divisions – or nomes – of Egypt; these nomes dated back to before Egypt's conquest by Alexander the Great in the fourth century B.C. The writing on most of the papyri, including this one, is in Greek. In A.D. 55, when this document was produced, Egypt was under Roman rule.

The second year of Nero Claudius Caesar Augustus Germanicus[13] Imperator, on the 6th of the month Audnaeus[14]=Sebastus,[15] at Oxyrhynchus in the Thebaid,[16] before the agoranomi[17] Andromachus and Diogenes.[18] Tryphon, son of Dionysius,[19] about ...[20] years old, of middle height, fair, with a long face and a slight squint, and having a scar on his right wrist, has bought from his mother Thamounis's cousin, Pnepheros, son of Papontos,[21]

13 Better known as the Roman emperor Nero.

14 A Macedonian month, roughly November.

15 Another term, of Roman origin, for the same month.

16 The nomes of Egypt were grouped into three large districts, of which the Thebaid was the southernmost.

17 Market regulators; one of the chief officials of the nome's capital town.

18 Both Greek names.

19 Both Greek names.

20 Word(s) missing.

21 All three Egyptian names.

Assumptions? This document was produced long before what has become the standard dating system of BC/AD (BCE/CE). People chose to date documents according to well-known terms of reference; the terms of reference the producers of the document use thus indicate what was well known and, presumably, of some importance. In this case, that appears to be the rule of the Roman emperor Nero.

Authority and **Groups?** This gives a little information about who in this society was seen as exercising authority: these officials, the agoranomi. It also looks like these officials presumably identified ethnically as Greek, given their names.

Groups? His name indicates that the buyer evidently identified as Greek, as did his father.

Relationships? We have a man identified as his father's son.

This kind of physical description in a legal document indicates that knowing who was who was not always easy in this time and place. Consider society today, with its social security numbers and photo identifications. Neither existed then. Note that this point answers none of the questions I have asked. No list of questions to ask of a source is ever likely to be complete. Or perhaps this discussion could answer the question about **Assumptions**...? Perhaps. One should in the end worry less about the category of conclusion than getting good conclusions themselves.

Relationships? Here Tryphon's mother is named, but not in order to identify Tryphon.

Relationships? Pnepheros, like Tryphon, is identified as his father's son, not his mother's.

Groups? These names are ethnically Egyptian. That indicates that Tryphon's mother's family identified as Egyptian. So, people who identified as Egyptians and as Greeks intermarried in Egypt at this point and could acknowledge that fact in an official document such as a bill of sale. It should be noted that the document does not specify these ethnic groups in any explicit way. Ethnic identity apparently did not have a legal bearing in what was a legal transaction, at least not in this one.

More physical description here, reinforcing the comments about challenges in identifying people noted above.

Groups? This indicates that women as well as men could own property and that a son could inherit from his mother.

Assumptions? This detailed description of what was near the house being sold and where on the street it stood indicates a society without street numbers. At least some streets had names, however: "Shepherds' Street."

Groups? Aha! Another indication that a woman – even with an adult son – could own property.

Relationships? It appears that we have relatives owning property in close proximity to one another. Perhaps family members liked to live near each other, or perhaps it was simply not a very mobile society.

Groups? Double aha! Further evidence of women owning property.

Copper, then, was valuable enough to be used as currency. But these buyers and sellers are not dealing in more precious metals as currency, like gold or silver. So, while the buyer and seller were wealthy enough to own a house, perhaps they were not rich? The descriptions of the physical appearances of the buyer and seller, noted above, would seem to confirm this; such descriptions might have been less necessary for better known, and so presumably better off, people.

The existence of the document suggests that a bill of sale was useful. For what? Presumably in case there was a later dispute as to whether the buyer really owned the house, the buyer (or his heirs?) could prove the buyer had bought it. Pnepheros's guarantee at the end bolsters this conclusion. That conclusion in turn indicates an expectation that there was a venue that might hear such disputes, such as a court of law. Again, unless it's **Assumptions?**, it's not clear that this discussion answers any of the questions asked above.

also an inhabitant of Oxyrhynchus, about 65 years old, of middle height, fair, having a long face and a scar above his …[22] eyebrow and another on his right knee, (the document being drawn up in the street) one half of a three-storied house inherited from his mother, together with all its entrances and exits and appurtenances, situated by the Serapeum[23] at Oxyrhynchus in the southern part of the street called Temgenouthis to the west of the lane leading to "Shepherds' Street," its boundaries being, on the south and east, public roads, on the north, the house of the aforesaid Thamounis, mother of Tryphon the buyer, on the west, the house of Tausiris, sister of Pnepheros the seller, separated by a blind alley, for the sum of 32 talents[24] of copper; and Pnepheros undertakes to guarantee the half share which is sold perpetually in every respect with every guarantee.

It's time to put the above comments in order, focusing on the most general questions, the ones to which all the aforementioned questions (both sets) are subordinate – those whose answers really get you to historical conclusions.

- *What conclusions can you draw from the source about the time that produced it? Do your answers to the prior set of questions – about who produced the source, etc. – in any way influence or limit what conclusions you can draw from the source?*

In first-century Oxyrhynchus in Roman Egypt, women could own property, even when they had living close adult male relatives, such as an adult son, because this source has several women owning houses (Pnepheros's mother, Thamounis, and Tausiris), one of them with a living son who was presumably an adult since here he buys a house. Men could benefit from women's ability to own property, as seen by Pnepheros's inheriting a house from his mother. But men seem to be identified as their fathers' sons rather than their mothers', so in that sense men were seen as more important. The only mother named here is Thamounis, apparently as a way of clarifying from whom Tryphon is

---

22 Portion missing.

23 A temple of Sarapis, a god created under the Pharaoh Ptolemy I out of aspects of Greek and Egyptian gods.

24 A unit of currency. Talents could also come in gold or silver.

buying his house. There is some indication that family members were interested in living near each other or that the society was not very mobile, given the locations of houses described here.

People with Greek and Egyptian names intermarried, so relations between the two groups may have been reasonably friendly. The fact that their ethnic identities are not mentioned suggests this aspect was of no legal significance, at least for this transaction.[25] A bit of evidence – the fact that the public officials (the agoranomi) had Greek names – may indicate, however, that people who identified as Greeks had higher status than Egyptians.

In drawing these conclusions, you should note that the evidence probably concerns people (with the exception of the agoranomi) who were not at the top of Oxyrhynchus society, as the purchase was made with copper rather than more precious metals, and the buyer's and seller's names were not enough to identify them, so their ages and physical descriptions, such as scars, height, and coloring, were noted too. The fact that one was Egyptian and that the Greek had Egyptian relatives – combined with the named agoranomi having Greek names – suggests a similar conclusion, reinforcing the impression that Egyptians were generally lower on the social scale than Greeks, but that Greeks could also require such identification. Or, to be more precise, people who identified as Egyptian were lower on the social scale than people who identified as Greek. While the source offers up these people's names, it does not provide certainty as to the ethnicity of their ancestors.

As to what the source shows about government: evidently people had property rights and there were courts that heard disputes over property. Otherwise, it's hard to see why this document would have been created. Some government officials had high enough standing that they were desirable witnesses, hence the two agoranomi who witnessed this document. It can also be observed that Roman emperors, though far away in Rome, were important enough and well-enough known to be used to date documents.

Since the source was preserved by chance, it does not appear that the interests of later generations make it misleading in the ways outlined previously. Literacy and the possibility that the document was produced by a legal expert may be a bigger problem in terms of bias. Consider, for example, the use of the year of the emperor's rule to date the source. Could that kind of familiarity with who was emperor and when have been more prevalent among the literate – it is not clear whether Tryphon and his relatives

---

25 The actual situation is a little more complicated than this, having to do with legal changes introduced by the Romans, a matter that is too complex for this book. But this fun fact in the end does not really affect this conclusion.

were literate themselves or had hired someone who could write – or more prevalent among those with legal training? From this document alone, it's impossible to say. At a minimum, however, one can conclude that members of the legal community in Oxyrhynchus could be expected to have been aware of who was Roman emperor and when that person ruled, and they could use that information to date documents.

Sources might answer some questions but not others. Notice that while some of the earlier questions are answered at least in part, some of the specific questions you might ask of a source, questions asked in the second round, simply do not pertain to this one:

- **Good and bad?** *Does the source make moral distinctions? If so, what is viewed as good? As bad? What values does the source seem to assume?*
- **Argument?** *If the source makes an argument, what is the argument about? What issues seem to be debated in this society? In what terms?*
- **Explain?** *Does the source attempt to explain anything? If so, how does it go about doing so?*

Finally, notice that many of the conclusions drawn here were not ones the author intended the source to convey. The writer had no intention of telling the reader about, say, relations between Egyptians and Greeks or the absence of paper identification in the Roman Empire. Historians often, even usually, use sources in ways that the producers of those sources did not remotely intend.

3.3 Reading against the Larger Historical Context

Here is another question you can ask of a source:

- **Representativeness?** *How representative is the source?* If you are reading this book, you probably won't be able to answer this question. To do so requires a lot of experience with sources and those from a particular time and place at that. For example, do you know if lots of documents from Egypt in this period use the emperor's rule for dating purposes, or is this one unusual in this regard? If the latter, then you can use the source to say that its author apparently expected future readers to know who the emperor was and when he ruled, but that this expectation may have been a false one. Because you are a beginner and do not know how representative a source is, most of your conclusions will have to be, in that sense, provisional. And that is fine. Ultimately you learn how to use primary sources by working with them. You have to start somewhere.

Finally, there is the related matter of the broader historical significance of the conclusions you draw. This is the big game. Understanding their broader significance is typically a matter of bringing to the source some knowledge of the time and place beyond the source itself. That knowledge sets an agenda. How so? Professional historians have usually read other historians' writing on the period from which a source comes. When they read primary sources, they are usually looking for evidence to confirm or refute conclusions drawn by those other historians or they are looking to answer questions prompted by their reading of those historians, questions they do not answer (more on this in chapter 7). In one way or another, other historians help create an agenda for a historian reading a primary source. When history students read primary sources, they are often doing something similar. The history student's instructor may have assigned secondary sources that prompt questions to ask of a primary source or the instructor may have discussed matters in class that do so.

Here are some general questions that address broader historical significance. Not all sources will lend themselves to all of these questions.

- **Larger questions?** *Do your conclusions have implications for your understanding of larger questions that historians have about the period you're studying?*
- **Cause or effect?** *Do your conclusions help you identify causes or effects of events or developments you've studied?*
- **Continuity and change?** *Do your conclusions imply change or continuity between the time that produced the source and earlier or later history?*
- **Relationship with the present?** *Do your conclusions imply change or continuity between past and present?* This is the only one of these questions that does not require you to bring some information about the past to the primary source. For example, you could conclude from this papyrus that ancient Egyptians, unlike people today, had to locate properties without the benefit of street numbers.

I have squeezed this little source pretty hard to get conclusions about Roman Egypt. (The commentary is longer than the source itself!) Even then, no reader can expect to squeeze every possible conclusion from a source.[26] But if your agenda as a reader of a primary source is set by reading other historians or by class discussion, then you are unlikely to squeeze quite so hard and get so many conclusions. Imagine that in class you learned about claims that after the Greeks conquered Egypt under Alexander the

---

26 For example, I have not said anything about the house being three storeys tall, which suggests that Oxyrhynchus may have been pretty built up – many modern communities have at most two-storey private residences. Other historians – or you – will also see conclusions that I have not.

Great in the fourth century BC, they formed a ruling class in the Hellenistic period (i.e., from Alexander's time until Roman domination in the first century BC) that worked to keep itself separate from the native Egyptians. Concluding, however, that people who identified as Egyptian and as Greek were intermarrying suggests either that what you learned in class was wrong or overstated or that in the Roman period that clear separation between ruling Greeks and ruled Egyptians weakened.

Or perhaps in class you learned that Roman emperors were distant figures to ordinary people in the Roman world, who lived their lives entirely in ignorance of them. Not so, indicates this source: at least people knew who ruled and when, or at least local legal specialists knew. Or perhaps your class focused on gender, in which case you have material about women and men, as discussed previously.

If, however, you are interested in Greek/Egyptian relations or awareness of the emperor, many of the conclusions drawn from this papyrus are not relevant (such as women owning property or family members living near each other) and so would not have been matters to consider anyway. And vice versa.

3.4 Documents of Practice

Much of this book's discussion of primary sources is organized according to different kinds of primary sources you might encounter. The title deed examined in this chapter is what might be called a "document of practice." This is a very heterogenous category; there is no tight definition of "document of practice," but this category generally has several characteristics. First, documents of practice were for practical use, usually immediately applied. In that way, they contrast with the treatises and literary sources discussed in chapter 5. Documents of practice also do not typically address a large audience, unlike the sources discussed in chapters 4 and 5. They may *also* be written for future generations, like the title deed discussed here, but they may not. Very often they do not make arguments, draw moral distinctions, or attempt to explain the world; this title deed does not. Such matters are more characteristic of the treatises discussed in chapter 5.

But just to illustrate the things that some documents of practice might do, consider a very flexible kind of source: letters. Letters are a very common historical source. They are also an attractive one. Barring recordings or film, they can be as close as one comes to hearing the voice of someone from the past. To read one is to feel like that past person is talking to *you*, more than the bill of sale just discussed. Letters are nonetheless subject to the same basic questions one should bring to any primary source.

Here is a letter. It was preserved along with the envelope in which it was sent, addressed to "Mr. MacArthur, MacArthur Headquarters, Kojimachu-ku, Tokyo." The return address reads "'Butsuko' [Japanese for "child of Buddha"] Asakusa Dōri [a street],[27] Tokyo, October 20, 1945." So, the letter came from someone in Tokyo, Japan. It was written early in the US occupation of the country after World War II. Indeed, the "Mr. MacArthur" to whom it was sent was General Douglas MacArthur, the American military governor of the country, among whose papers the letter is preserved. It is translated from the Japanese.

I state to Mr. MacArthur:

Congratulations on Your Excellency's bountiful happiness.

Ordinarily I am one who breaks down the barriers of nationality, and I even smiled at reports of Your Excellency's high praise for American soldiers. But on the night of October 17 at 7 P.M., I was in the women's side of a public bath on Asakusa Dōri [avenue] in Mukō Yanagihara 2-chōme[28] – a person bombed out by the war, washing away the day's toil from my tired body – when a commotion began: "An American soldier is peeping." I could not believe that an American soldier with any intellectual pride would do this, but I happened to see your country's soldiers taking turns laughing and peeping from a small window by the side of the bath. If your excellency were to hear about this incident, I knew you would be deeply aggrieved, and I secretly felt sorry for you. You have said that Japanese soldiers may have done so and so,[29] and I do not wish to negate your words, but not all of the young Japanese men sent to the front were uncivilized. There were many who were capable of human reflection and cherished refined aesthetics. Your excellency, please bear in mind that there are some among your soldiers who have the lowest tastes. Women of your country and my country too are all God's children. I pray the best of health to you.

Butsuko

The **Who?**, **What?**, **Where?**, and **When?** here are obvious. The matter of **Audience?**, however, is often especially pronounced in letters. While some letters are addressed to the general public (think of what is called an "open letter"), most letters are addressed to an individual. Knowing who that addressee is, as here, puts you in a good position to think about what the writer wanted the letter to accomplish.

---

27 This section of Tokyo has a well-known Buddhist temple.

28 A district in Tokyo.

29 On October 16, MacArthur had in a public announcement criticized the conduct of Japanese troops during the war, contrasting it with the behavior of US forces.

In this case, one has a mini-narrative of events: some American soldiers peeping at Japanese women in a bathhouse. You might want to draw some conclusions about that: perhaps that American soldiers during the occupation could feel immune from punishment for bad behavior toward the occupied or that bathing in Japan might be done in a bathhouse rather than at home, and such bathhouses were sex segregated. The fact that the letter was sent to MacArthur suggests a determination to get the general to discipline his troops. The matter of **Groups?** here is also obvious: Japanese (women) and American (men). While the writer nowhere makes that request, the contrast she draws with MacArthur's account of the behavior of American and Japanese troops as well as her assertion that women in Japan should be regarded in the same terms as women in the United States suggest a call to action as well as a rebuke. Perhaps the indirectness of this letter also suggests that Japanese people, or perhaps Japanese women, were not so comfortable making such complaints directly. How much that was a matter of Japanese culture and how much derives from Japan's status as an occupied country is, from the letter alone, unclear.

This chapter has examined a sample primary source and raised questions you can ask of any primary source and others you can ask of many sources. It has also discussed questions that apply to some primary sources but not others. The chapter concluded with a second genre within the class "documents of practice" – letters. The next chapters will address various categories of primary sources and questions that are particularly appropriate to each.

chapter four

Narrative Sources and Cognate Sources

Narrative sources tell a story. Unlike literary sources (on those, see chapter 5), the story they tell purports to be true. They are arguably the most traditional kind of source for historians. At first glance, they can also appear the simplest. In fact, they are often the most difficult.

Consider, for example, this newspaper account of a double murder in New Orleans, published in the New Orleans *Item* on May 23, 1918. The place to start is answering **Who?**, **What?**, **Where?**, **and When?**: it's a newspaper article written May 23, 1918, by an unnamed reporter for the *Item* in New Orleans. As for **Audience?**, it's the newspaper-reading public, then a large segment of the population. It would be easy to draw conclusions from this source by simply summarizing the story it tells. The result might be something like: Joseph Maggio and his wife, a middle-aged couple who owned a grocery, were murdered with an axe in New Orleans on the night of May 22, 1918. Two of Joseph's brothers said they found the bodies. The Maggios' safe had been opened. The panel of an outside door had been cut out and the door's lock unscrewed. The police held the brothers as material witnesses, but the police were also uncertain as to who had committed the crime and why.

But other questions arise:

Reliability? As you will see, the prior narrative basically reproduces the facts recounted by the source. Could the reporter have been a bad reporter and so have gotten things wrong? Could he – given the date, it probably was a "he" – be a biased reporter and consciously or unconsciously misreported the story?

Sources? *Where did the source get its information?* The writer is presumably getting his or her information from somewhere. Knowing where may also help you judge the source's reliability.

The New Orleans *Item*, May 23, 1918

COUPLE HACKED TO DEATH WITH AX IN SLEEP

Joseph Maggio and Wife Slain in Grocery Store During Night

BROTHER OF MAN IN NEXT ROOM HEARD GROANS

He, With Another Brother, Held By Police as Witnesses: Only Evident Motive Robbery

For the past six years Joseph Maggio, a native of Sicily, has run a small grocery at 4901 Magnolia street, corner of Upperline.

It was a typical establishment of its kind – the grocery in the front and the rooms of Maggio and his wife in the rear. In one of them there also lived Maggio's brother, Andrew, a barber.

The grocery served a small and mixed clientele, half black and half white. Probably its receipts were not enormous, and they were sufficient to keep Maggio and his wife in comfort, and to allow them a little extra margin for investment. They got along well with their rather variegated trade – so well that they enjoyed a sort of neighborhood distinction. To a half dozen squares[1] Maggio's store was "the store" and its proprietors were "Mr. and Mrs. Joe."

Had No Known Enemies

So far as known they had no enemies. Born of a farming class, they had attained the distinction of owning a small business – the ambition of nine out of every ten immigrants of their class. They had been married fifteen years. Rather unusually, they had no children – sufficient cause for dis-agreement in many Italian families, but apparently not in this. Both were of middle age – Maggio, 45; his wife, 35. Altogether a commonplace, con-tented couple, with a long and peaceful life presumably ahead of them.

At 5:30 o'clock, Thursday morning the police of the seventh precinct station received a telephone call from Andrew Maggio, the brother, who roomed with the couple. They should come to Upperline and Magnolia at once. His brother and sister had been killed.

---

1 A New Orleans term for "blocks."

[Margin note:] **Theme?** It looks like the writer wants to make the reader sympathetic to the Maggios: they were not piling up huge sums, but they did well in a small business and were liked by those who knew them.

[Margin note:] **Theme?** Again, the writer implies they had worked hard for what they had – starting as farmers or farm workers and then setting up a small business. The couple got on well with each other, despite a childlessness that for other couples spelled trouble.

A squad, headed by Captain John M. Dunn, commander of the station, and Corporal Joseph W. Condo answered the call. They found the bodies of Maggio and his wife lying side by side in bed, the throats and heads of both cut open by repeated blows of an axe.[2] The man, apparently, had been killed instantly. The woman had time to put out an ineffective hand, which had been cut half-way through. The story of a wholly murderous intent was told by the fact that, of the dozen blows struck, all but one or two would have been sufficient to kill. But the murderer had wanted to make sure.

Axe Found in Bathroom

In an adjoining bathroom was the axe, blood covered. Behind the dresser was the strong box, which, presumably, had contained Maggio's valuables. It had been forced open and rifled of its contents. Some of them lay on the floor, among them two Liberty Loan bonds, – proof of the small investment margin which had been the fruit of the couple's industry, and two Red Cross pledge cards, both of the present campaign issue. Whatever money there was had evidently been taken by the murderer.

Theme? The writer uses the bonds to point out the couple's hard work.

Waiting for the police were Andrew Maggio, Jacob Maggio, another brother who runs a shoe repairing shop at 1638 Magnolia, and Salvatore Maggio, who has a grocery at 4638 Clara street.

They told their story, Andrew beginning it. His room was separated from that of the murdered couple by a four-inch partition. They were still up when he had gone to bed Wednesday night. About 4:30 o'clock in the morning he had been awakened by some noise – he was not sure what it was – and, listening, had heard groans from the bedroom of his brother and sister-in-law.

Strong Box Was Rifled

He had listened a moment, but had heard nothing else. He had then gotten up and knocked at their door – an inside door which connected with his room. Receiving no answer, he had run down the street to the home of his brother Jacob, a block away. Jacob had joined him, and, together, they had gone after the third brother, Salvatore. Then all three, after spending about a half hour in gathering sufficient numbers to make the venture safe, had returned to the house and broken the door.

---

2 The articles in this chapter do not always spell "axe" consistently (compare "Ax" in the headline of this one).

Sources? So, it looks like the police are a source for the writer. That would of course be natural.

Sources? Presumably Joseph Maggio's brothers were also sources for the reporter.

Sources? Having the police's point of view confirms the reporter had spoken with the police.

Everything had been as the police saw it.

That was the story of Andrew and the other brothers. The rest of the tale was told by two bodies, the rifled strong box, the blood-stained bed, and added to these, two other factors. A panel in a rear outside door had been cut out, and furnishing the murderer a means of entrance and a portion of an inside door lock, apparently unscrewed by the slayer, it was lying on the floor near the inner door from which it had come.

This was the material with which the police had to work. Otherwise the brothers could give virtually no clew[3] to the slaying. The axe was one which belonged to the family; it had been lying in the backyard the night before. So far as they knew, their brother had no enemies. No Sicilian vendetta had pursued him to America. He had been happy in his domestic life. All had been going on well, they said; then had come this.

Two Brothers Held as Witnesses

Sources? Aha! There may be a problem with concluding that the reporter spoke with the brothers. If the brothers were in police custody, they were presumably not available to the reporter. The police could be the source of what the brothers had to say – to the police.

Sources? This information presumably comes from the police.

After investigating, Captain Dunn ordered two of the brothers, Andrew and Jacob, held as material witnesses. Both were subjected to a rigorous cross-questioning all morning, but it brought out nothing which threw any considerable light on the double murder. A half dozen detectives have been assigned to the case, however, and developments are looked for at any time.

"There are a number of points that have to be explained," said Captain Dunn, in discussing the circumstances of the killing. "It is strange that so brutal a murder could have been committed in an adjoining room without awakening Andrew Maggio. It is peculiar that he should have gone after his brother before investigating further, and that the two should have gone after the third brother before doing anything. The only explanation is that they were actuated by fear, and it seems funny that two men should have been such cowards.[4]

Search is being made by detectives for the explanation of an apparently meaningless message, scribbled in chalk on a sidewalk at Magnolia and Robertson. The writing was not observed until about five hours after the murder. It reads:

"Mrs. Joseph Maggio up tonight – just write. Mrs. Tony."

The sentence is considered of possible importance only in its relation to one of the police theories – that the murder was committed by an insane

---

3 I.e., "clue."

4 The end of the quotation is not marked.

person. The inclination, however, is to regard it as the work of a practical joker with a perverted sense of humor.

Insane Man Possible Murderer

"There are some other things, also, which may have not yet been explained, but which may be later. Investigation has just begun, and the crime is an unusually mysterious one. Maggio may have had enemies of which his brothers did not know. He may have been reputed to be quite wealthy. The murder may have been committed by an insane man; it is brutal enough. There are any number of possibilities. Meantime, we are holding the two brothers merely as material witnesses. It is too early in the investigation to accuse anyone."[5]

Sources? More information from the police.

Assistant Superintendent Capo arrived on the scene with the coroner.

[Caption to picture:][6] Hacked to Death in Bed With Ax

JOSEPH MAGGIO AND WIFE, who were murdered in their Magnolia Street home and grocery during the night, while brother of Maggio slept in adjoining room. Rifled strong box may indicate motive, although police confess considerable mystery surrounding double slaying.

There is nothing here that particularly suggests the reporter is unreliable; he is sympathetic to the victims, but it is not evident that that sympathy would lead him to misrepresent the facts. Clearly, one of his sources – perhaps his main source – is one or more police officers. And presumably the police were at least as well informed as anyone except the murderer. No reason is evident for the police to mislead, so the account appears reliable as to the facts summarized previously.

Of course, it is always possible that more than one source will concern the same thing. Historians sometimes call such sources "cognate sources." In this case, for example, a police or autopsy report concerning the Maggios would be a cognate source. Unfortunately, neither survives. But other, narrative, cognate sources do. When you have cognate sources, comparing them allows you to ask some more questions:

Agreement? *On what matters do they agree?* Such agreement helps bolster their reliability, at least on those matters where they concur.

---

5 The article does not identify who is quoted here.

6 Although the newspaper articles in this chapter included pictures, I have included only the captions and descriptions of those pictures.

Contradiction? *On what matters do the sources contradict each other? Such variance undermines their reliability, at least on those matters where they counter each other. Can you identify why one source might be more worthy of belief on such matters versus the other?*

It turns out that there are other primary sources regarding the Maggio murders. Here is another newspaper story, published in the New Orleans *Statesman* on the same date:

New Orleans *Statesman*, May 23, 1918

CHALK NOTE ON WALK IS ONLY CLEW IN MURDER

Mysterious 'Mrs. Toney' Is Brought Into Maggio Double Tragedy

The *Statesman* knows which detectives found the chalked message. That suggests the police are a source for this reporter.

At 12:30 o'clock Thursday afternoon Detectives Obitz and Dodson found the following message written in chalk on the sidewalk at South Robertson and Uppperline streets, just a few squares from the scene of the murder.

Contradiction? The *Item* rendered this message as "Mrs. Joseph Maggio up tonight – just write. Mrs. Tony." While it's not entirely clear what either version means, they don't seem to mean the same thing.

"Mrs. Joseph Maggio is going to sit up tonight. Just write Mrs. Toney."

It was within two squares of the Maggio place that Louis Werner, convicted murderer of Patrolman Frank J. Connor, shot to death his brother-in-law, Charles Singleton.

At Magnolia and Valence streets – just three squares away – William P. Kaiser shot and fatally wounded Edward Munch following a fist-fight. Kaiser was sentenced to five years for manslaughter.

Theme? The *Statesman* frames the story differently from the *Item*. The context here is other homicides in the neighborhood, implying that the neighborhood is dangerous.

One of the most ghastly murders recorded in this city in many years was committed just before dawn Thursday morning when Joseph Maggio, a grocer and saloonkeeper of Upperline and Magnolia streets, and his wife, Mrs. Katherine Stabile Maggio, were butchered with an axe in their bedroom adjoining their place of business.

Robbery was the motive, but so far as concerns the identity of the person or persons responsible for the atrocious crime, the case is a mystery. It is not believed the murderers secured much money, since the murdered man on Wednesday deposited $650 in the bank as shown by his bank book – the largest deposit he has made at one time since the first of the year.

Mr. and Mrs. Maggio slept alone in their bedroom overlooking Upperline street. They had no children. A brother of the murdered man, Andrew Maggio, aged 28, who occupied quarters in the adjoining half of the house, discovered the crime at 4:45 o'clock. At that hour, he heard his brother moaning loudly and rapped on the wall. Receiving no response, and afraid to enter his brother's room alone, he hurried to the home of another brother, Jake Maggio, 4638 Magnolia street, and together they entered the death chamber.

Woman's Body on Floor

Lying diagonally across the bed, with his feet touching the floor, was the body of Joseph Maggio. On the floor alongside the bed and resting across the feet of her husband, lay the dead body of his wife. The floors and bed were smeared with blood. The man was not yet dead. Jake Maggio summoned the police, while Andrew telephoned for the Charity Hospital ambulance. He died shortly after the arrival of the internes from the hospital.

The three brothers of the deceased, Andrew, 28, Salvadore, 33, and Jake, 36, were closely questioned by the police. Andrew, the youngest, is unmarried. He is a barber in Camp street, near Julia. Monday he is to report to the exemption board office for examination in the army draft call. Salvadore conducts a business similar to his dead brother at 4638 Clara street – two squares from the dead man's residence. Jake is a cobbler.

Entrance to the Maggio home was effected evidently by scaling the fence, the gate being found intact, as well as all outer doors and windows. The murderer or murderers then chiseled away the panel of the door leading from the yard to the kitchen and then unscrewed the lock. The intruders secured Maggio's axe which stood against the back of the house in the yard. With the blade smeared with blood, the murderous weapon was found by the police under the bathroom, which is situated between the kitchen and the bedroom where the butchery was committed.

Superintendent Mooney and Captain Capo cannot understand why it was that the noise, which the murderers must have made in chiseling away one of the heavy door panels of the outer door, did not awaken the sleeping couple.

That the persons responsible for the butchery were familiar with the lay of the premises, is indicated by the fact that every physical fact shows that the intruders were bent upon only one purpose – that was to get to the bedroom of Mr. and Mrs. Maggio, for it was in a corner of that room the combination safe was kept.

Overlook Valuable Jewelry

Another fact that is puzzling the police is that the safe was in no way mutilated, it either having been left open or the murderers were cognizant of the

Agreement? Sources? The two accounts agree on who discovered the bodies, with a slight difference. The *Item* makes clear that Andrew is the ultimate source of this information. The *Statesman* does not make this clear.

Agreement? Here the *Statesman* confirms the *Item*'s details about the outer door and the lock, clarifying that it was a kitchen door.

Contradiction? The *Item* says the bloody axe was found in the bathroom. Here the axe is found under it – perhaps meaning under the house?

Sources? More evidence of the police as a source.

Agreement? The accounts agree that the safe was open and imply money was taken. But there is a difference in interpretation. The *Statesman* is much more confident that robbery was the motive for the crime.

combination. Brothers of the dead man say they believed he always kept the safe under the combination.

Contradictions? The *Item* put their years as 45 and 35, respectively. It may be that one reporter or the other – or both – are getting their information from not-well-informed neighbors. Presumably the police would have been better informed. Notice that in each set of dates, the husband was older, which may suggest something about expectations regarding married couples.

[Photograph of the Maggios, with caption:] "MR. AND MRS. JOSEPH MAGGIO, aged 39 and 36 years, respectively, hacked to death with an axe while in bed in their room adjoining the grocery and bar, Upperline and Magnolia Sts. Robbery appears to have been the motive. The case is a mystery so far as concerns the identity of the culprits. The photograph was taken at the time of the Maggios' wedding fifteen years ago."

Other Murders Committed In the Vicinity of the Scene of the Maggio Act

A tin box, where Maggio usually kept his money, was found mashed and open alongside of the dresser. How much money was in that box will never be known. It is believed, however, that it contained the only receipts of Wednesday's grocery and saloon sales, which possibly did not amount to more than $50. A jewelry box, encased in a stocking, had been placed by the dead man under the safe. This was found to be intact. It contained jewelry valued at several hundred dollars.

Theme? Again, this writer put the crime in the context of other murders in the neighborhood.

The Maggio murder and robbery is similar in many respects and recalls two previous cases of recent date. On May 19, 1917, Vincent Miramon, dairyman of Washington and Hagan avenues, was pounded on the face and head with a hammer and died in the Charity Hospital a few days later. A Negro was arrested for that crime but no evidence could be secured upon which to base a conviction. A few months ago, an Italian grocer and saloonkeeper several squares away from the Maggio home and grocery was hacked with a hatchet, similar to the Maggio case, but recovered. The place was robbed. As in the Maggio case, one of the wooden panels of the kitchen door was chiseled out.

Sources? This indicates the reporter has spoken with the police.

Chief of Detectives George Long, who is credited with much ingenuity in running down crime, especially of the sort committed Thursday morning, was placed at the head of a squad of detectives by Superintendent Mooney in an effort to find some clew that might lead to the murderers.

Theme? The writer again brings up other New Orleans murders, those which he or she says were similar to the Maggio case. He or she does not, however, claim they took place in the Maggios' neighborhood. Also note the names of the other victims: all Italian, a point that will become more significant below.

New Orleans some years ago recorded a veritable epidemic of such cases. Among the more prominent was the Cruetti case, the Sciambra case, and the Rosetti case. There were several others within the past decade. All of these cases remained mysteries.

Police Thursday morning searched in vain for blood-stained garments. Instructions have been given to keep certain persons well known to Maggio under surveillance because of the fact that the evidence has a tendency to show that the crime was committed by persons well acquainted with the home surroundings and habits of the murdered couple.

The Maggio grocery, saloon and residence is located in a sparsely settled location of the city. Vacant lots dot the neighborhood, and it is considered an ideal place for such a crime. This too, is a fact as regards the neighborhood surrounding the residence and home of the grocer and saloon keeper of Panola and Dublin streets, where a similar crime was committed and as regards the surroundings of the scenes of some of the other crimes enumerated. In most cases the victims were Italians. Besides the three brothers in New Orleans, the murdered Italian has a mother and sister who are in Arkansas.

Married 15 Years Ago

Mr. and Mrs. Maggio were married here fifteen years ago. Mrs. Maggio, who was Miss Katarina Stabile, came to this country about eighteen years ago with her aunt, who is now said to be in New York City. She had no other relatives in this country.

The theory that the murder and robbery was the work of negroes, of which there are a great number in that neighborhood, is not countenanced by police.

Photographs of the death chamber were taken shortly after the discovery of the crime by John Norris, chief Bertillon operator and his assistant, Maurice O'Neal.[7] These photographs will be produced at the trial, in the event of an arrest. The pictures will be held as records in the Bertillon office.

So, the *Statesman* confirms major points of the story told by the *Item*: Joseph and Katherine Maggio – the *Statesman* adds the wife's name – were murdered on May 22, 1918. The safe was open and the outside door (now said to be a kitchen door) had a panel cut out and the lock unscrewed. Some details get no confirmation, such as Andrew and Jacob Maggio being held as material witnesses, although the *Statesman* does say the police thoroughly interrogated them.

---

7 In the later nineteenth century, Alphonse Bertillon devised a method of measuring and recording the features of a human being, the better for police to identify a suspect if that person had been measured on some previous occasion.

Margin notes:

Sources? Further indication that the police are a source here.

Theme? And yet another reference to other crimes. And a statement that most of the victims were Italians.

Sources? Yet more confirmation that the police are a source here. But who has suggested that Black people committed the murder? Could it be neighbors? And if so, did the reporter get this information from them? Or did the reporter learn of the speculation from the police, who also rejected it?

There are also some contradictions, such as where the axe was found and the exact text of the chalk message. What to make of those contradictions? It would be most natural to conclude that these differences reflect different sources of information, although who those sources were is unknown to us. Or was some information simply garbled in transmission?

Of course, it is also true that one source for both papers was the police. That fact weakens the force of the agreement between these newspaper articles. It is possible that details like the chiseled door panel, the lock, and the safe all came from one source: the police. If so, you could argue that those details are no more likely to be correct for being reported in two newspapers than in one. On the other hand, if the police were the source of those details, at least they were consistent in giving them out or reporters were consistent in hearing them: both reporters produced the same story on that score.

But what about those discrepancies? One can note that they are both easy things to get wrong. "Under the bathroom" compared with "in the bathroom": it's easy to imagine a reporter hearing one and writing down or remembering the other. Of course, that fact does not help decide which story got it right. The chalked message is a matter of getting a short text exactly right: a mistake is easy. That might especially have been the case if the reporters had not read the message itself, but heard it stated orally by a police officer. If the reporters did get the message from the police, this could have been because of laziness, a lack of caution, or maybe a lack of access to the original (perhaps it had been erased?).

While the reporter clearly has a theme – the Maggio murders should be thought of in terms of a larger pattern of crime – it is hard to see how this would lead to false or distorted reporting of the facts of the case.

But the *Statesman* was not the last newspaper to cover the Maggio murders. The next day, the New Orleans *Times Picayune* published the story. One can ask the same questions of it as of the *Statesman*.

The *Times Picayune*, May 24, 1918

[Caption of map of the house and of photograph of Joseph Maggio and his wife:] Scene of Latest New Orleans Murder

From a photograph taken on their wedding day fifteen years ago, and the house in which they were killed while asleep in their bed

BROTHER'S RAZOR INVOLVES HIM IN DOUBLE KILLING

Weapon Found Beside Bodies of Maggios, May Lead to Charge of Murder

Police last night uncovered clews which they declare point to Andrew Maggio, a barber, as the slayer of his brother and sister-in-law, Joseph

Maggio and his wife, in their bedroom early Thursday morning at Magnolia and Upperline streets, where they conducted a barroom and grocery.

Early investigation indicated the victims had been hacked to death by an axe. Careful examination of the bodies several hours later, however, showed the murderer had cut the throats of Maggio and his wife with a keen instrument, then had beaten their heads with the axe to cover traces of the real death weapon.

In the bedroom was found a blood smeared razor. Andrew Maggio conducts a barber shop in Camp Street, near Julia. The police announced Esteban Torres of 123 South Rampart Street, a barber in Andrew Maggio's employ, had identified the razor as one which Andrew Maggio had removed from the shop a day or two ago, saying he wanted a nick honed from the blade.

An apparently important development.

FORMAL CHARGE LIKELY

Andrew Maggio and another brother, Jake Maggio, had been held all day at the Seventh Precinct station pending investigation following their statement they had discovered the double crime at 5 a.m. Confronted with the blood-stained razor Thursday night, Andrew Maggio showed signs of nervousness, according to the police. Formal charges probably will be lodged against him Friday, the police said.

Agreement? This confirms the *Item*'s account that the police held the brothers, although the *Times Picayune* does not give being material witnesses as the reason.

Theme? The theme here is much more an essential part of the story than in the two earlier accounts: Andrew Maggio was the murderer.

The following inscription, written crudely with chalk on the sidewalk, was discovered at noon Thursday by Detectives Obitz and Dodson at Upperline and Robertson streets, a block away from the scene of the crime: "Mrs. Joseph Maggio is going to sit up tonight just like Mrs. Toney."

Sources? The police are a source for this reporter.

Contradiction? And yet a third version of the chalked message!

The writing is legible and resembles that of a schoolboy. The theory is entertained by detectives the sentence was written by an accomplice of the murderer or murderers to warn them that Mr. and Mrs. Maggio would be on their guard Wednesday night. "Mrs. Toney" is thought to be a woman who foiled the slayers in an attempt to kill her. The police are confident they will clear the mystery if they find the writer.

Sources? The reporter has been getting information from the police.

Sources? The police as a source again.

Robbery is regarded by the police as the only plausible motive for the crime. A safe in Joseph Maggio's room was found open and rifled of its contents. There were no indications of the vault having been forced open, although Joseph Maggio's brothers say he always kept it locked and he was the only one to their knowledge who knew the combination.

Agreement? Here is the open safe again.

Sources? Again, the Maggio brothers are a source, but it is unclear whether the reporter has spoken with them directly or their statement comes via the police.

APPEAR FAMILIAR WITH HOUSE

This strengthens the police in their belief the slayer or slayers were familiar with the Maggio household and probably were on intimate terms with

Sources? The police are a source again.
Theme? This would fit with Andrew Maggio being the murderer.

the murdered couple. Beneath the safe detectives found a box, wrapped in a stocking, which contained several hundred dollars' worth of jewelry which apparently had not been touched. The box was evidently put there by Joseph Maggio and had been overlooked by the robbers.

The receipts of the day before, about $50, are thought to have been all the money in the safe, as Joseph Maggio's bank book shows he deposited $650 in the bank Wednesday, this being the largest deposit he made this year.

Andrew Maggio, who lived in the other half of the house occupied by Joseph Maggio, and Jake Maggio, 4638 Magnolia street, told the police they discovered the crime shortly before 5 o'clock Thursday morning. Andrew gave the following account:

Sources? If Andrew Maggio was in custody, it seems unlikely this came directly from him, quotation marks or no.

"I was awakened by a noise in my brother's room, which is opposite mine. I heard a noise like someone groaning and knocked on the wall, but got no answer. So I went outside and called to Joe at the bedroom window on Upperline street, but still received no answer. I then knew something was wrong. But I went for Jake and he came back with me. We entered together and saw what had happened."

The crime is said by detectives to be one of the most gruesome in the annals of the New Orleans police. Husband and wife had been struck in the head and face with an axe. Mrs. Maggio's head was almost split open, and her husband's had a gash in it several inches long. The bed was smeared with blood which also spattered the floor.

MAGGIO ALIVE WHEN FOUND

Maggio lay on the bed, his feet resting on the floor. He was still alive when found. Mrs. Maggio lay on the floor beside him, dead.

The husband died shortly after the arrival of the Charity Hospital ambulance.

Agreement? and **Contradiction?** So the *Times Picayune* supports the *Item* on where the axe was found.

Agreement? This source also confirms the removal of a panel in the kitchen door and removal of the lock.

Theme? Although this point was made in the earlier articles, given the finger pointing at Andrew Maggio in this one, all this looks bad for Andrew. Could he have murdered the couple and then chiseled out the panel in order to make it look like an outside job? **Sources?** Clearly the police.

It was Joseph Maggio's axe with which the crime was committed. Detectives found it covered with blood, in the bath room.

The dead man and his wife were insured, and the policies made out each in other's names are in the possession of the police. Captain Dunn of the Seventh Precinct station said Andrew and Jake Maggio declare they have no interest in the policies, as their mother, in Arkansas, is now the beneficiary.

Detectives investigating the case believe the murderer or murderers entered the premises by scaling the Upperline street fence. A panel of the kitchen door was chiseled away and the lock removed. How this was done, however, without arousing Joseph Maggio, his wife or Andrew Maggio was a feature of the case the police could not understand.

"It's a queer case," Captain Dunn said Thursday evening. "To hammer on a chisel certainly makes a noise, especially on a door. The fact that Mrs. Maggio was found on the floor leads me to believe she jumped up after her husband was struck, and was killed while trying to defend him."

Chief of Detectives Long was assigned by Police Commissioner Mooney to handle the case.

Less than an hour after the police were notified, Andrew and Jake Maggio were taken to the Seventh Precinct station, where they were questioned closely, and ordered held for investigation.

Joseph Maggio and his wife, natives of Italy, had been in this country fifteen years. His three brothers, Jake, a cobbler; Salvatore, grocery and saloon keeper two blocks from Joseph's place, and Andrew, a barber, came to the United States several years later. Jake had been notified to appear for examination Monday in the draft call.

So, where does this third account put the historian? First, the facts. There is further confirmation of some facts, although one still has the problem of suspecting they may all be coming from the same source. And there is yet another discrepancy: a third version of the chalked message.

There is also some further information, most notably implicating Andrew Maggio as the murderer. The police thought he was guilty at this point; they expected to charge him. That in turn may have influenced what facts the police were giving out – the oddity of a door panel being chiseled out without waking anyone and in particular the bloody razor. It is not surprising that this would have formed the theme of the *Times Picayune* story. Readers would want to know who the murderer was, so this was an angle that would appeal. If a newspaper has any motive, it is to sell newspapers. In this sense, one would expect some bias against any suspect. The fact that the *Times Picayune* was the first out with a clear suspect would have made having a suspect that much more attractive.

There is another approach: Does one of the stories hold together better than the others? Does one simply seem to make more sense? In this case, there is not much to choose among them. They largely say the same things, although they frame those things differently. But on one point, each differs from the others: the message in chalk. Here are the versions:

Item: "Mrs. Joseph Maggio up tonight – just write. Mrs. Tony."
Statesman: "Mrs. Joseph Maggio is going to sit up tonight. Just write Mrs. Toney."
Times Picayune: "Mrs. Joseph Maggio is going to sit up tonight just like Mrs. Toney."

On the face of it, the last of these seems to make the most sense on its own terms: May 22's murder victim is going to sit up tonight just like a previous victim. So that gives the *Times Picayune* a little more credibility, at least as an accurate reporter of facts if not as an interpreter of them. There is still, of course, the mystery of who chalked the message and why. (The police seem ultimately to have concluded that it was something of a nasty joke, done after the murders and not by the murderer. Perhaps it was the comment of a neighbor, who would have known about both attacks.)

Indeed, *was* Andrew Maggio the killer? Given these sources – particularly the last one – he looks guilty. But facts develop. The police reinterviewed Esteban Torres and showed him three razors found in Andrew Maggio's room. Torres found them as much like the razor Andrew had taken home as the bloody one presumably used in the murder. Moreover, although Andrew's recruiting his brothers is odd, it would also be odd that he, alone in the house, and so with the time to do it, would not have made certain Joseph Maggio was dead before bringing them to the scene.

Widening the lens – and looking beyond these three sources – suggests that Andrew was not the culprit. The murder appears to be one of a series committed by a killer who came to be known as the "Axe Man of New Orleans." The Axe Man attacked Italian grocers who lived by their shops, like the Maggios, in the wee hours of the night. He typically broke in by chiseling a panel out of an exterior door and killed using an axe found in the yard; most people had axes in the days of wood stoves. And he walked without shoes in the houses he entered, presumably to move silently, sometimes robbing his victims, sometimes not. Indeed, footprints of stockinged feet were found on the freshly varnished counter in the store. Narrative sources – any sources – can deceive. If they have a program – a theme – that drives the narrative, the danger is even greater.

But there is a way around that deception. One can "read against the grain."[8] In other words, the historian reads for apparently incidental details, things that the writer appears to assume are unremarkable, even about which the author may not have even really thought at all. Such reading against the grain may tell one what people at the time thought was normal, even if the writer were deliberately lying about the central subject of the story – in this case, a double murder. (This book has in fact done some reading against the grain already. Recall the discussion of the dating clause of the bill of sale in chapter 3.)

Consider, for example, the fact that we have an immigrant couple who own a small business. Or that somebody assumed that Black people must be responsible for the crime. Or that this was apparently a racially mixed neighborhood – which means there

---

8 Note that in literary studies, "reading against the grain" also involves identifying a writer's assumptions, but it is only a step to challenging those assumptions in some way.

were racially mixed neighborhoods. Or that it does not appear to have been unusual for shopkeepers to live at their stores. "Reading against the grain" in this way can reveal a lot – usually about society and culture.

It can seem as though there is not much to do with a narrative source but replicate its narrative. Not so! Reading against the grain alone suggests that. Moreover, multiple sources for the same thing enrich each other. That may especially be the case when using narrative sources to produce, well, a narrative.

chapter five

Literary Sources and Treatises

5.1 Literary Sources

History is an interpretative art. So is the study of literature. In both, students draw conclusions about what they read. And, indeed, the first job of students of literature and history is the same: to understand in a literal way what the source says. These commonalities often trip up beginning history students because often their only previous experience in drawing conclusions from texts is for the purpose of literary rather than historical analysis. While these two modes have things in common, their aims are ultimately rather different. One reads in a literature class in order to understand what one reads at a deeper level, perhaps in some way that will reveal truths about oneself or one's society, perhaps simply to understand something about the work, perhaps in order to relate the work to other literature one has also read – but the deeper level is the goal. Even when literary scholars pay attention to the historical context of a work, it is usually in order to use that context to understand the work better, not to use the work to understand the historical context better. The focus is the work of literature itself. The historian, however, reads primary sources ultimately to draw conclusions about the world outside the source, the world that produced it. Minimally, that world would be the mind of the person who produced the source, but usually one wants to go wider, to get at the society, culture, or circumstances that led that mind to think what it thought and so write what it wrote. So, for the history student, the primary source is simply a means to an end, an end that lies very much outside the source itself. Literature – fiction – can be useful in reaching that end.

Yet, fledgling history students are often misled by their prior study of literature to assume their goal is that of literary study. If while reading a primary source, you find yourself coming to conclusions about what the source "means to me," you are probably engaged in literary analysis. The history student asks instead "what did the source mean to the person who produced it?" or "what did the source mean when it was produced?" (Notice the past tense.) Forget what the source means to you. While historians may ultimately want to uncover the implications of the past for understanding the present – and oneself – that work comes later, not when drawing conclusions from the source itself.

The confusion of literary and historical approaches to a text is especially common when the primary source concerned is a work of literature. Historians often use literature as primary sources: for some periods and places, that is all that survives aside from material evidence. Indeed, the analysis done by literary scholars is often useful to historians when dealing with such sources. The temptation to engage in literary analysis when using such sources can be especially strong. Resist it.

To illustrate, consider the following literary work, asking the basic introductory questions of any source outlined in chapter 3.

The Pañcatantra, Book III, Story 7: The Brahman, the Thief, and the Ogre[1]

What? This is a story from a collection of short stories.

Audience? Presumably Hindus.

Where? India.

When? Ca. 300 BC–AD 500. **Literacy? Audience?** At this point, most people were illiterate. So the audience, in addition to being Hindus, was probably fairly elite.

Who? We don't know who wrote it.

Audience? One learns a bit more about audience here: it was wide, albeit confined to the literate. *Perhaps* the original audience was expected to be rulers.

The Pañcatantra *("Five Books") a Hindu work translated here from Sanskrit, was produced in what is now India; it is a collection of very short tales, most of them about animals. The text states that these stories were recounted by a wise man to three not-very-bright sons of a king, who wanted his sons to learn to be effective rulers. The* Pañcatantra's *date is very uncertain, perhaps ca. 300 BC, but possibly as late as ca. AD 500, when it was translated into another language. The work itself says it was written by Vishnu Sharma, but many scholars believe that person is a fiction. Written long before the printing press, it survives in a number of copies, which suggests it was widely read. Some scholars have suggested that because the* Pañcatantra *presents itself as told to a king's sons, that it was written for rulers, but it could well be that that self-presentation is itself a fiction.*

Once a certain poor brahman[2] received a present of a pair of cows, which had been brought up from calves by feeding with ghee, oil, salt, grass, and [other] wholesome foods, so that they were very fat. And a certain thief saw them, and he thought as follows: "This very day I shall steal them." So he started out in the early evening, and as he went along some unknown person touched him on the shoulder. Whereupon he asked in alarm, "Who are you?" And he spoke truthfully: "I am a night-roaming brahman-ogre.[3] You also tell me who you are." Said he: "I am a thief." And when the other asked again: "Where are you going?" he said: "I intend to steal a pair of cows

---

1 *The Panchatantra*, trans. Franklin Edgerton (South Brunswick, NJ: A.S. Barnes and Co., 1965), 123–4.

2 Hindu society was divided into certain hereditary groups or castes. The Brahmans, or priestly caste, had the greatest prestige.

3 I.e., an ogre, who lived on human flesh, who had in an earlier life been a Brahman.

from a certain brahman. But where are you going?" Then being reassured by this information the brahman-ogre also said "I too have started out to seize that same brahman." Then they went thither both together and stayed side by side, waiting for the proper time. And when the brahman had gone to sleep the brahman-ogre was creeping up to seize him first; when the thief said to him: "This is not the right way. After I have stolen his two cows, then you may seize him." Said the other: "That too would be wrong. Perchance the noise of the cows might wake him, and then I should have come in vain." The thief said: "If when you seize him he gets up and make an outcry, then everybody will be roused; and then I cannot steal his two cows. So I will steal the cows first, and afterwards you may eat the brahman." As they were disputing with one another they got angry, and with their rivalry they straightaway woke up the brahman. Thereupon the thief said: "Brahman, this brahman-ogre wants to seize you." But the brahman-ogre said: "This thief wants to steal your two cows." Hearing this the brahman got up and being put on his guard saved himself from the ogre by reciting the mantra[4] of his sect's deity, and saved his two cows from the thief by brandishing his cudgel. So both the thief and the ogre ran away.

Preservation? No evidence here indicates who preserved this work and why.

Meaning? This is a harder question – and a big one. *What is the author trying to communicate?* If there is a moral to the story, perhaps it's that being too determined to have one's way may result in losing what one hopes to gain or that cooperation is more productive than selfishness. It is best to test how strong such a conclusion is by proposing alternative meanings and seeing how well they hold up against one's first conclusion. Here's another possibility: it's good to be equipped, with a mantra and a cudgel, in order to defend oneself. Both are possibilities. But there's a problem here; one could imagine a much shorter version that would make the latter point: that a Brahman-ogre and thief assail a Brahman with two cows, and the Brahman successfully defends himself and his cows by reciting a mantra and using a cudgel. This conclusion would have no need for the complication of a conflict between the Brahman-ogre and the thief. So it's probably wrong.

So what to make of this meaning? Well, at the very least, it suggests that it made sense to someone in India between ca. 300 BC and ca. AD 500. And the fact that there were many copies of this text suggests it was accepted by many literate people. So, the meaning was acceptable to the culture more generally. But there is a caution here: different people can take different meanings from a story. Perhaps that was the case here? The text itself

---

4 A sacred stanza.

provides no evidence on the matter. Later commentaries on the *Pañcatantra* might. And, of course, you should bear in mind that this is one story of many in the *Pañcatantra*. That larger context may change that meaning. But if the tale of *The Brahman, the Thief, and the Ogre* is all you have, then best not to worry overmuch about that possibility in a class.

There is another approach, one that can be particularly helpful with literary texts. Instead of worrying about what the author is trying to communicate (the "meaning" of the text), concentrate on what the author assumes to be normal and natural – or at least possible and calls for no special comment. This approach is sometimes called "reading against the grain" (on this, see also chapter 4). If the author makes such assumptions, the audience presumably does too. So what is to be learned from *The Brahman, the Thief, and the Ogre* by reading in this way?

The Pañcatantra, Book III, Story 7: The Brahman, the Thief, and the Ogre

Once a certain poor brahman[5] received a present of a pair of cows, which had been brought up from calves by feeding with ghee, oil, salt, grass, and [other] wholesome foods, so that they were very fat. And a certain thief saw them, and he thought as follows: "This very day I shall steal them." So he started out in the early evening, and as he went along some unknown person touched him on the shoulder. Whereupon he asked in alarm, "Who are you?" And he spoke truthfully: "I am a night-roaming brahman-ogre.[6] You also tell me who you are." Said he: "I am a thief." And when the other asked again: "Where are you going?" he said: "I intend to steal a pair of cows from a certain brahman. But where are you going?" Then being reassured by this information the brahman-ogre also said "I too have started out to seize that same brahman." Then they went thither both together and stayed side by side, waiting for the proper time. And when the brahman had gone to sleep the brahman-ogre was creeping up to seize him first; when the thief said to him: "This is not the right way. After I have stolen his two cows, then you may seize him." Said the other: "That too would be wrong. Perchance the noise of the cows might wake him, and then I should have come in vain." The thief said: "If when you seize him he gets up and make an outcry, then everybody will be roused; and then I cannot steal his two cows. So I will steal the cows first, and afterwards you may eat the brahman." As they were disputing with one another they got angry, and with their rivalry they straightaway woke up the brahman. Thereupon the thief said: "Brahman, this brahman-ogre wants to seize you." But the brahman-ogre said: "This thief wants to steal your two cows." Hearing

Our Brahman is poor! This does not sit well with how most people envision members of a higher class. So, here we have evidence that the common picture that Brahmans were wealthy needs at least qualification. Moreover, this Brahman is imagined herding cows himself.

Here we have what is assumed to be a good diet for cows in early India. It explains why the cows are fat, and so why the thief wants to steal them. The first three ingredients might surprise modern farmers.

This confirms that Hindus believed in reincarnation.

---

5 Hindu society was divided into certain hereditary groups or castes. The Brahmans, or priestly caste, had the greatest prestige.

6 I.e., an ogre, who lived on human flesh, who had in an earlier life been a Brahman.

this the brahman got up and being put on his guard saved himself from the ogre by reciting the mantra[7] of his sect's deity, and saved his two cows from the thief by brandishing his cudgel. So both the thief and the ogre ran away.

So, sacred texts can have power over supernatural beasts.

Another question is often pertinent to literary sources, one that is closely allied with **Meaning?**: *Is there a theme?* In other words, is there some repeated idea, especially one that the author finds various ways to bring up. In the case of this story, there does not seem to be one. But the tale is very short, so there is not much scope for repetition. If you read more stories from the larger work, perhaps some themes would emerge.

5.2 Treatises

A treatise attempts to convey information to very explicitly and systematically persuade the reader to adopt certain conclusions. Treatises can be a point of entry into what people in an era thought about the treatise's topic. But they pose dangers too. In particular, since a treatise is intended to persuade, it may be a key to what people of a past time did *not* think – and so the author thought they needed persuasion to believe – rather than represent generally accepted thinking. In either case, however, a treatise does represent just that: thought. Treatises are perhaps most traditionally used by historians for intellectual history – that is, the history of ideas. Minimally, the existence of a treatise with certain ideas indicates that at least *somebody* had those ideas. For this reason, there are times that intellectual history reads like an explication of treatises. Indeed, students can be especially tempted to merely summarize such sources when doing history with treatises. Resist that temptation.

So, let's take a portion of a treatise from fifteenth-century France. Most of the standard beginning questions can be answered from the introduction or title:

Who, what, where, when? The source was written by Christine de Pizan ("of Pizanno") at the court of the king of France between September 1408 and ca. 1430. It's a treatise on warfare and chivalry.

Audience? The chapter title indicates it's aimed at rulers, or at least those around them. The fact that Christine lived and worked at the French court strengthens this conclusion. So does the fact that she wrote in French; Latin was reserved for the clergy, for bureaucrats, and for a few lay intellectuals. It should be said, of course, that if Christine was not able to write in Latin, this argument is a no go.

---

7 A sacred stanza.

Literacy? Literacy was the preserve of a minority in this period. So the source presumably reflects a learned perspective. And who else, of course, but an educated person is likely to write a treatise?

Preservation? There is no evidence here to bear on the question.

Meaning? Meaning is such a big issue for a treatise that it is best dealt with in the running commentary on the source.

To this, one should add some other basic but second-round questions that are likely especially to pertain to treatises:

Authority? *What or whom does the source seem to view as authoritative?*

Good and bad? *Does the source make moral distinctions? If so, what is viewed as good? As bad? What values does the source seem to assume?*

Argument? *If the source makes an argument, what is it? What issues seem to be debated in this society?* In the case of a treatise, argument and meaning generally come down to the same thing.

Explanation? *Does the source attempt to explain anything? If so, how does it go about doing so?*

In addition, the last approach described for literary sources in 5.1 also often applies to treatises:

Assumptions? *What does the author assume to be normal and natural – or at least possible and calling for no special comment?* Since a treatise usually makes an argument, these will very likely be the assumptions from which the argument starts.

Themes? To this one can add a question raised regarding literary sources: *Are there some running themes, perhaps not spelled out?*

As will be evident in the commentary, some of these questions overlap!

Christine de Pizan, *The Book of Deeds of Arms and of Chivalry*, Part 1: chapter V: Considerations a King or Prince Should Entertain in Initiating War and the Points of Debate He Should Keep in Mind While Deliberating the Matter[8]

Christine de Pizan (1364–ca. 1430) was born in Italy but moved to France as a child with her father, a servant of the king of France. Once widowed, she began to write to

---

8 Christine de Pizan, *The Book of Deeds of Arms and of Chivalry*, ed. Charity Cannon Willard, trans. Sumner Willard (University Park, PA: Pennsylvania State University Press, 1999), 18–21.

support herself and her children. Like most professional writers of the time, she made a living not by selling books but from support by wealthy people who appreciated what she wrote. Members of the royal family and nobles at the court of the French king were her chief patrons. The work was written after September, 1408, as that is the date of the latest event to which it refers. Although she wrote in French, it is thought that she probably read Latin.

As it is licit for a prince to engage in wars and battles, pursuing them for the reasons mentioned above, and as these are great and weighty matters that touch the lives, blood, and the honor and the fortunes of an infinite number of people, it is necessary to look closely into the matter, for without such a look no such thing should be undertaken, nor should it be undertaken by anyone without experience. That one should hesitate to undertake war even on someone weaker there are numerous demonstrations. What great blows the African power dreamed of, or the proud city of Carthage, its capital, and the Spaniards, not to mention the very powerful King Antiochus, lord of a great part of the East who led so many into battle that with their frightful elephants the affair was quickly finished. Then there was the mighty King Mithradates, who was sovereign of twenty-four powerful countries and even of the whole world, but even these could not and did not subdue the very slight power of the Romans.[9] For this reason, nothing that is in the power of fortune should be risked lightly, for no one can know which side will be favored.

Therefore, it is necessary for the prince to be wise, or at the very least be disposed to use wise counsel, for as Plato[10] said, fortunate is the country where the wise govern, as Holy Scripture[11] also testifies. There is absolutely nothing that so needs to be conducted with good judgment as war and battle, as will be seen later. No mistake made in any other circumstances is less possible to repair than one committed by force of arms and by a battle badly conducted.

What then will the wise prince upon whom it is incumbent do when, for any of the reasons mentioned, he must undertake wars and fight battles? First of all, he will consider how much strength he has or can obtain, how many men are available and how much money. For unless he is well supplied with these two basic elements, it is folly to wage war, for they are necessary to have above all else, especially money. Whoever has enough and wishes to use it can always find plenty of help from others, even more than he wants; witness the wars in Italy, especially Florence and Venice, that are commonly fought more with their

Meaning? Rulers should be wary about deciding to go to war because war can harm a lot of people and even the side that appears stronger can lose. There are some historical examples of the latter.

Good and bad? and **Assumptions?** War needs to be justified. Those justifications appeared in a section of the source you do not have here. But Christine also thinks rulers are supposed to value their peoples, who can be damaged in war.

Authority? Christine looks to the past for examples, drawing them from ancient Roman history.

For now, just note this mention of fortune's power and unpredictability.

Authority? An ancient Greek philosopher and the Bible are authorities for Christine.

Meaning? So, for these reasons and because warfare itself requires good judgment, and because an error in war is hard to correct, the ruler needs good advice when deciding on war.

Meaning? A wise prince must consider how strong he is in soldiers and money: it's foolish to go to war if you don't have enough. Money is especially important because one can always hire soldiers. And trying to get more money out of one's people than they can pay will make enemies at home, which is worse even than the enemies abroad that the prince would attack. To repeat a point, even foreign enemies who seem weak may not be that weak.

Assumptions? Christine takes it for granted that warriors will be men.

---

9 All the states Christine mentions in this paragraph went to war with Rome and lost.

10 The Greek philosopher (427–347 BC).

11 I.e., the Bible.

Assumptions? Princes cannot just confiscate money from their subjects willy-nilly. Their good will is needed or at least desirable.

Assumptions? Subjects should give money to the ruler by consent. Here, Christine seems to think it's possible for the ruler to seize the money without it – but she still thinks it will dangerously alienate those from whom he seizes it.

Themes? This is the second time Christine has mentioned fortune's unpredictability – maybe there is a theme here. Indeed, in the next sentence, she gives an example of fortune being on the side of the underdog.

Authority? Another example drawn from ancient Roman history.

money than with their citizens.[12] For this reason they can scarcely be defeated. So it would be much better for the prince, if he does not consider that he is supported by money from the treasury, or by rich subjects full of goodwill, not to conclude any treaty with his enemies if he feels threatened with invasion, or to undertake to begin a war if he lacks the means to carry it on. For it is quite certain that if he begins it in the hope of extracting more from his subjects than they will be able to bear, and without their consent, he will merely increase the number of his enemies. It will profit him little to destroy enemies from outside in order to acquire them nearby and in his domain. It should be remembered that the prince must not underestimate the power of any enemy, however slight it may appear to him, for he cannot know what fortune another will have in his favor. It is written of a shepherd named Briacus[13] that fortune was so favorable to him that she sustained him in power with a great number of thieves and pillagers he had assembled to fight Rome, powerful as it was, for a period of more than fourteen years. Much grief he brought to them, and he defeated them several times in battle, nor were they able to destroy him. His life was ended by one of his own men, who killed him.

Therefore, in order that such things might not come about, the prince will assemble in council the four estates of his realm,[14] which should be summoned for such a purpose. That is to say, the elder nobles and experienced men at arms, who know how to organize and attack; also the law clerks,[15] for in the laws are set forth the cases in which a just war can be undertaken, along with several examples of these; also the burghers,[16] for it is necessary for them to participate in the organization, since they would need to take charge of fortifying towns and cities, and also to persuade the common people to help their lord. Additionally, there should

Assumptions? Once again, Christine assumes that money is something subjects need to consent to give the king. Perhaps for her, one advantage of getting advice from the assembled four estates is an opportunity to persuade them to give that consent. Perhaps this is why craftsmen should be honored by having them attend?

be some representatives of the craftsmen, the more to honor these people. They must be carefully approached so that they will be the more inclined to help the lord financially....

In this tradition the good and wise King Charles, fifth of the name ... saw that the English were keeping badly the agreements of the peace treaty he had concluded with them.... So the aforesaid king, in view of the fact that he had been obliged to agree to a dishonorable treaty, one that even the English did not keep,

---

12 At this time, Italian city states commonly hired companies of mercenaries.

13 Briacus, also known as Viriathus (died 139 BC), led a rebellion against the Romans in what is now Spain.

14 Medieval sources typically refer to France having three estates: the clergy, the nobility, and everyone else.

15 I.e., lawyers, who are called "clerks" here because they tended to be members of the clergy.

16 I.e., greater and wealthier citizens of the towns.

and for other reasons too long to explain, assembled in his parliament in Paris the aforementioned four estates....[17] This council, after long deliberation concluded that there was due and just cause to begin the war again.

So, what to make of these observations?

For one thing, it is evident that warfare and the politics of war were of sufficient interest that a woman would be willing to write about them. That does not mean, of course, that women typically acted as warriors – Christine assumes in passing that warriors will be men.[18]

There are only a couple of instances in a short selection, but there seems to be a theme here: the unpredictability of fortune was much on Christine's mind. This in turn suggests that she lived in a rather disordered world, where changes in fortune were common. Of course, this could also perhaps reflect her personal circumstances: a mother who, at the royal court, presumably lived well but, as a widow, was forced to support herself at a time when most women of her station did not have to make a living.

Christine seeks authority in Roman history, ancient philosophy, and the Bible. It's tempting to suggest from simply counting instances that Roman history is more important for her than the other two.

Christine seems to see money as foremost among the resources a ruler must draw on in war.[19] But how to get it? The prince does not appear here as an all-powerful tyrant. Rather, he must obtain funds from his subjects through consent or persuasion. The avenue to do this is an assembly of the four estates, which advises the king on various aspects of whether to go to war. But this discussion leaves a puzzle. The notes indicate that French kings did indeed consult an assembly of estates – namely three estates: clergy, nobility, and everyone else – when making large decisions about war and levying taxes. But de Pizan's four estates do not line up with the three estates

---

17 In her earlier biography of Charles V, de Pizan describes Charles as having summoned a council of the nobles, clergy, and townspeople on this occasion.

18 And to bring in some outside information: indeed, Joan of Arc, who fought for the French crown and was Christine's contemporary, was a rare exception.

19 To bring in more outside information: in fact, this fits well with what else is known about France in the late Middle Ages. War was becoming increasingly expensive and kings were relying less heavily on their vassals (i.e., warriors who held land from the king in return for military service) in war. Money for mercenaries, equipment, and much else was essential.

known from a number of other sources. So what to make of this? There are several possibilities:

1. Christine did not know there were customarily three estates or what they were. This, however, seems unlikely for a woman who a) lived at the royal court and b) took an interest in the politics of her time (seen in this selection by her reference to mercenaries employed by Italian cities).
2. Historians are wrong about the three estates. But there is plenty of evidence for the three estates, more than appears regarding Christine's four. So, this possibility is also unlikely.
3. Christine was not in fact *assuming* assemblies made up of four estates, as suggested in the running commentary above. She was *advocating* for a change to four estates, structured along the lines she lays out. And she projected that arrangement back into the time of King Charles V to give it the credibility of having a precedent, thus contradicting her own earlier account of the assembly. Of course, this last detail relies not on this source itself but on another: her earlier biography of King Charles V of France (see note 17).

Given these facts, this third possibility seems the most likely. It also contains a moral. While one might try to identify what an author assumes without thinking (and so to read against the grain), it is also the case that authors can sometimes be very inexplicit about an agenda and yet quietly follow it.

Finally, another observation about the relationship between rulers and the ruled: Christine clearly believes that the good of subjects should weigh on the minds of rulers. One can imagine people who believed otherwise – for example, that the decision whether or not to go to war is a matter of the ruler's personal honor. She, however, sees the ruler as having duties to the ruled.

Literature and treatises often present the most complex problems when it comes to determining their meaning. So getting at their meaning can be especially demanding. In the end, however, historians typically go beyond that effort in order to use such sources, like any sources, as keys to the larger world that produced them.

chapter six

Material Evidence and Comparing Sources

6.1 Introduction

Primary sources come in two broad categories: written evidence, on the one hand, and material evidence, on the other. Traditionally, historians have focused on written evidence; this book does too. Increasingly, however, historians have been concerning themselves with material evidence. Such evidence can, in turn, be divided into two overlapping categories. The first has been, and still is, primarily the province of archaeologists: the leavings of daily life, such as bits of pottery, buildings and the foundations of buildings, bricks, and tools. Such material can also include items not directly produced by humans but which can still inform the archaeologist about the conditions in which people lived. Preserved pollen, for example, allows conclusions about what kind of food people grew in the past. Art is a second category – paintings, sculptures, buildings, photographs, posters, postcards, flags, cartoons, and so on. Traditionally, "high" art (such as paintings and sculpture) has been the subject matter of art historians, whose field is considered distinct from that of simple historians; art historians have in recent years also increasingly studied what could be called "low" art: more ephemeral objects, such as cartoons or postcards. Both archaeologists and art historians receive specialized training regarding the material with which they work. These categories are also not mutually exclusive: archaeologists and art historians alike are quite capable of studying, for example, jewelry. While some historians have embraced archaeological evidence in the past decades, a larger phenomenon has been historians working with evidence that is more traditionally studied by art historians. Why? Perhaps it's because such evidence is often, although not always, less technically challenging.

6.2 Art

In any case, one needs to ask of art the same basic questions one asks of any primary source: **Who? What? Where? When?** In many cases, however, beginners will have to get the answers to most of those questions from the publication that includes a picture of the source or the exhibit that includes the item. Consider, for example, figure 6.1.

Now the **What?** you might be able to tell just by looking: look at the dimensions and the fact that the short side on the left lacks fringes. This is a flag. Most readers would be able to answer the remaining basic questions only by reading an introduction to the image. Only if you happen to be acquainted with the Asofo (also spelled "Asafo") flags of Ghana are you likely to see that this is an Asofo flag of the Fante, one of the peoples of Ghana. Asofo (literally, "war people") companies were local Fante militias that preceded the arrival of British colonizers in the mid-nineteenth century and which now also carry on various social service functions as well. The **Who?** will almost certainly require information from outside the source. This Asofo flag was made by Kweku Kakanu (ca. 1910–1982), who had a long career of designing such flags; only the very expert have the connoisseurship to identify by the style whether a flag was produced by Kakanu. **Where?** has already been answered, again, not from the source itself: Ghana. **When?** The presence of the Union Jack – the flag of Great Britain – in the upper-left corner suggests that the flag must date between the mid-nineteenth century and 1957, when Ghana gained its independence. (Asofo flags produced after 1957 typically carry the Ghanaian flag in the upper left.) Other evidence beyond the object itself indicates a more precise date: ca. 1935. One point perhaps worth noting is that companies commissioned new flag designs when they got a new commander. **Audience?** was presumably anyone who viewed the flag, both the Asofo company itself and anyone else when it was displayed publicly. The matter of **Preservation?** is unclear; the flag was acquired by the Smithsonian Institution from a New York art dealer in 1984. Since the flag does not bear writing, the matter of **Literacy?** does not arise.

What about **Meaning?** The Union Jack suggests an acknowledgment of British affiliation. What about the rest? Then and now, Asofo companies competed with each other for prestige, even engaging in armed conflict. The crocodile evidently represents this company itself; its viewing the fish in the water recalls a Fante proverb: "Fish grow fat for the benefit of the crocodile," the fish being rival Asofo companies. Indeed, Asofo flags often refer to Fante proverbs, which increases the chances that this one does. An additional or alternative meaning is that the pond and its inhabitants – including the birds? – refer to the sacred bodies of water that Asofo companies were charged to protect. In this case, the company aims to defend the fish, not to eat them. *If* the first meaning is correct, it supports a conclusion that the competition among companies could

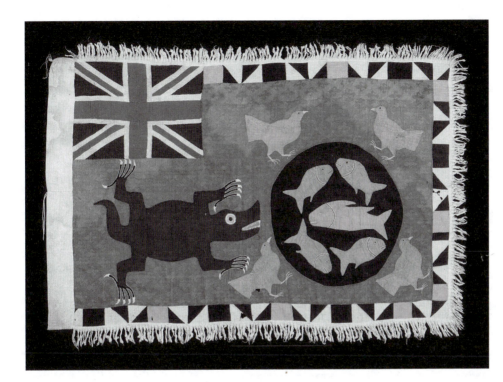

Figure 6.1 *Asafo flag, Ghana.* Kweku Kakanu, Fante artist. Circa 1935. Commercial cotton cloth. H × W: 108 × 152.4 cm (42 1/2 × 60 in.). Museum purchase 88-10-1. Photograph by Franko Khoury. National Museum of African Art, Smithsonian Institution.

be very much "in your face." (Indeed, a nineteenth-century observer remarked that Asofo flags were sometimes designed to insult other Asofo; even recently, flags have provoked conflict between companies.) But there is ambiguity here – as there often is when it comes to the meaning of art.

The presence of the Union Jack is likewise somewhat ambiguous. Clearly it indicates in some sense an acceptance by this Asofo company of affiliation with the British Empire. But what to make of that affiliation? In much of colonial Africa, Britain exercised "indirect rule," keeping chieftains and other authorities in place and governing through them. This flag could be used as evidence that the British had co-opted the Asofo companies in the same way. Could the presence of the Union Jack indicate the acceptance by this Asofo company of this arrangement? Perhaps. It is also true, however, that the colonial authority required its approval for the design of Asofo flags. So the company was not free to adopt whatever design it wanted; the Union Jack may have been required, although there is some evidence that Britain regulated Asofo flags in order to tamp down conflicts among the companies. The flag shows that this company accepted its British affiliation, but the degree of its acceptance – grudgingly? neutrally? enthusiastically? – is not indicated by the flag itself.

This discussion of the Union Jack, the crocodile, the pond, and the fish concerns "iconography": the meaning of visual elements of a work of art and how they relate to the world outside the work. So, an important part of asking about **Meaning?** is asking about **Iconography?** *Do elements of the work have iconographic significance and if so, what?* Here, the Union Jack is a good example of iconography.

Then there is the matter of different cultural influences in the work. (For an example of such questions, see chapter 8). So, **Multiple cultures?** *Does the work incorporate elements from more than one culture?* This question pertains to the flag. It is a Fante flag, but it has been argued that the very use of flags was adopted by the Fante from European practice after direct European contact in the fifteenth century. If this is true – and it has also been noted that flags were known from an earlier period among other African peoples – the very existence of the flag indicates that the Fante took on a European practice for their own purposes. And again, there is the Union Jack in the upper left.

6.3 Comparing and Contrasting Sources

It can help with any source to compare and contrast it with another. When doing so, one can ask about **Style?** *Is the work's style or way of representing the world different from works of other periods or places?* Consider figure 6.2, a painting of King Louis XIV of France and his family, painted by Jean Nocret (1670), and figure 6.3, Edwin Landseer's painting (done in the 1840s) of Queen Victoria of England, her husband, the Prince Consort, Albert, and their daughter.

Iconography really helps with Nocret's painting. First, Louis is identifiable not only by his face but also by his scepter; he is also the only figure clothed in gold. Louis himself was always associated with the sun, so, like the Greek sun god, Apollo, is crowned by a laurel wreath. The woman standing to Louis's right is his mother; she is depicted as having a crescent moon on her head – and so is represented as Cybele, the Greek goddess who, as Mother Earth, was mother to the gods. Louis's brother, seated at the left, bears a torch with a star-like flame – a Greek symbol of the morning star, which goes before the sun but is lesser than it. Indeed, in court ceremonial, it was Louis's brother who woke the king every morning. The other figures are family members depicted with other symbols identifying them with other Greek mythological figures. The presence of cherubim – child angels – reinforces the royal family's heavenly standing. Given its iconography, this painting clearly celebrates royal authority. It also stresses the connection between the members of the royal family and the king; it makes sense that Louis's brother commissioned it.

This conclusion about royal authority becomes stronger when one compares Nocret's painting with that of another royal family – Landseer's painting of Queen

Figure 6.2 Jean Nocret, "King Louis XIV of France and His Family." © RMN-Grand Palais / Art Resource, NY.

Figure 6.3 Edwin Landseer, "Windsor Castle in Modern Times." Royal Collection Trust / © Her Majesty Queen Elizabeth II 2020.

Victoria and Albert, commissioned by Victoria herself. The style here is rather different from Nocret's painting. No iconography identifies the couple with the gods or even as royalty. Albert is seated before a hunting dog and dead animals lie before the couple. Hunting was a masculine activity; one can conclude that Albert is just returned from the hunt – indeed, he still wears his hunting boots. Their daughter is picking up one of the dead birds. The house dogs (Victoria did indeed keep dogs like this) are, not surprisingly, also very interested in Albert's catch. The scene, in other words, is domestic, one that might be found in any upper-crust house, although – a kind of departure from realism – presumably game would not actually have been brought into such a well-appointed room. Strikingly, Albert is rather casually seated while Victoria – the reigning monarch and so Albert's legal and social superior – stands, appearing to wait on him. This certainly fits the time's gender expectations of wives being subordinate to their husbands. And in contrast with Albert's masculine hunting boots, Victoria is dressed for the indoors and holds a small bouquet, a feminine touch. Here is a royal family that is depicted as more family than royal. The contrast between this painting and Nocret's clarifies the meaning of each.

A stylistic difference relates to whether the painting relies on iconography. The ancient Greek iconography discussed above is echoed by the appearance of bare-chested and bare-legged men in Nocret's work. In other words, Nocret is depicting his seventeenth-century figures in the style of ancient classical art – a real contrast with the greater realism of Victoria and Albert's painting. So the stylistic difference – one more realistic and less dependent on iconography, one less realistic and more iconographically oriented – is clear. Here is the beginning of a case that artistic styles changed between the seventeenth and nineteenth centuries.

What historical conclusions can one draw from these paintings? One might stress the countries from which they come, concluding that monarchy was more exalted in France than in Britain. Or one might stress the times in which these works were produced and conclude that monarchy in the seventeenth century was more authoritative than in the nineteenth. Or perhaps that it was easier for people to think of a male monarch (Louis) as having more authority than a female one (Victoria). Or one could focus on the apparent association of the chief female subject in Landseer's painting with the home and the only male subject with the outdoors. In any of these cases, the matter of how **Representative?** the works are (of their time, place, or depiction of the women and men) is important and of course cannot be concluded just from the evidence here. What should also be evident is that drawing conclusions from material evidence is as hard, perhaps harder, than from written evidence.

In discussing these paintings, I have compared and contrasted them. You should notice that the similarities (these are both paintings of royal families) are worth noting, but these likewise highlight the contrasts (the use of iconography and lack of it, the domesticity of one scene compared with the other, etc.). Note that the contrasts reveal more than the similarities. That is usually the case when doing history. This discussion thus leaves a final question: **Compare and contrast?** *What similarities and differences do you find between the two sources? How can similarities be used to highlight contrasts? What do the contrasts reveal about the contexts that produced the sources? (Or how can you explain the contrasts?)*

6.4 Archaeological Evidence

While art historians specialize in works of art, archaeologists specialize in less glamorous material remains of the past – although they too can concern themselves with works of art, an area where archaeology and art history overlap. Historians sometimes look to archaeological evidence as a supplement, to fill in where written sources are absent – a habit that can annoy archaeologists. Archaeology can reveal the past quite independently of written sources. For both reasons, however, historians have become more interested in archaeological evidence in recent decades – recall the artifacts discussed in chapter 1.

As another example of how archaeological evidence can be used, consider figure 6.4: an amphora. These containers were used to ship goods, typically liquids, all over the ancient Mediterranean and beyond it: this one was dug up in Baldock in the 1960s, in southeastern England after a bulldozer revealed the site while digging for a new road. Amphorae survive in many, often subtly different, kinds. In 1899, archaeologist Heinrich Dressel published forty-five numbered, distinct types (customarily referred to according to "Dressel numbers"); many more types have since been identified. The Baldock amphora turns out to be a Dressel 1a amphora – see figure 6.5, sketch labeled "1."

The questions **Who?**, **What?**, **Where?**, and **When?** still apply. For **Who?**, many Dressel 1a amphorae were produced over a long period of time; that kind of consistency implies experienced, likely professional potters. **What?** has already been dealt with: a Dressel 1a amphora. As to **When?**: the key here is knowing approximately when Dressel 1a amphorae were made; unfortunately, they do not bear dates. But enough such amphorae have been found in enough sites along with other, more datable objects, or in sites that can be dated by written evidence, that one can say this kind of pot was produced in roughly the first half of the first century BC.

Where? has a couple of answers. The amphora was found at Baldock: easy enough. But where was it made? That answer requires more explanation. A number of Dressel 1a amphorae bear brief inscriptions called *tituli picti* that suggest they come from the west coast of southern Italy.

Figure 6.4 Amphora found at Baldock, England. North Hertfordshire Archaeological Museum.

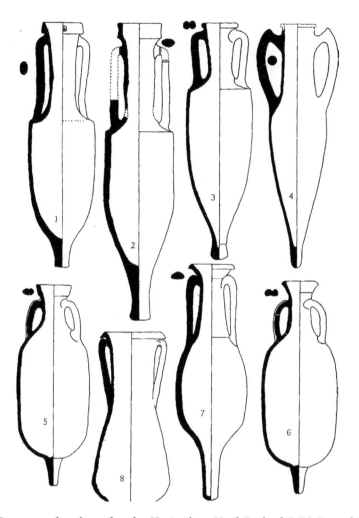

Figure 6.5 Fragments of amphorae found at Heningsbury Head, England. D.P.S. Peacock, "Roman Amphorae in Pre-Roman Britain," in *The Iron Age and Its Hill-forts: Papers Presented to Sir Mortimer Wheeler on the Occasion of His Eightieth Year, at a Conference Held by the Southampton University Archaeological Society, 5th–7th March, 1971*, ed. David Hill and Margaret Jesson (Southampton: Southampton University Archaeological Society for the Department of Archaeology, 1971), fig. 35 (p. 163).

But there is other evidence, even without this abbreviated written evidence. **What is the source made of?** This question can be asked of art and of written sources. For example, medieval texts were written on parchment or animal skins. What kind of animal skin – cow? sheep? – and how many animals can tell you something about, for example, the economic resources of the producer of the manuscript. But the material composition of objects comes up especially often in archaeology. Close examination of Dressel 1a amphorae under magnification reveals their "petrology": they are made of clay containing elements such as garnet (fragments too tiny to be valuable or even likely much noticed by their makers), volcanic rock, and so on. These combinations – three have been identified for Dressel 1 amphorae – again tie them to what is known of the soils on southern Italy's west coast. There is a good chance that this vessel and many others were used to carry wine; later written evidence suggests the region had a reputation for fine wine. (And sometimes chemical analysis uncovers the contents' residue.)

What about larger conclusions? The presence of this amphora in Britain indicates that there was at least some trade, direct or indirect, between southern Italy, then under Roman rule, and Britain before Rome conquered it in the 40s AD. In fact, the Baldock amphora is one of many Dressel 1 pieces found in Britain's southeast. Like most ancient pottery, most of these survive in pieces, or "sherds," as archaeologists call them. Indeed, the Baldock amphora was found in sherds too; look at the lines in figure 6.4 that show where the pieces were glued together. The types are so well known that well-trained archaeologists can often tell to what Dressel type even fragments belong, like those found in England at Heningsbury Head (see figure 6.5).

So, many Dressel 1 amphorae are found in southern and southeastern England. Map 6.1 shows where they were, indicating that those parts of England had good trade contacts with Rome even before the Roman conquest. Written evidence from the time does not reveal this, but humble sherds do. Did these Britons like fine south-Italian wine?

But to return to the Baldock amphora: one can be more precise about **Where?**, as it was found in a man's grave, buried alongside high-status goods, and so this was a man of some standing, perhaps a tribal chief. This circumstance helps explain why the entire amphora could be recovered so many centuries later. The placement of the Baldock amphora in this grave also suggests that Britons before the Roman conquest valued Roman goods, perhaps even some aspects of Roman culture. For a high-status man to be buried with a Roman amphora seems to reveal at least this Roman good as a high-status item. Knowing what amphorae were made for may make this seem rather like choosing to be buried with a really big mason jar; Romans in southern Italy might have thought so too. But Britons apparently thought differently.

That is a very interesting and large conclusion, but is it true? As always, one should consider alternative conclusions the evidence might support. Perhaps this amphora was included in the grave not as a sign of status but as a comment on – or even a celebration of – the dead man's capacity for alcohol. Here **Representativeness?** can be important. If more graves of high-status Britons include Roman amphorae, then this amphora is not so idiosyncratic, and so it was not a comment on an idiosyncrasy like the deceased's drinking habits. If this amphora is unusual, however, then it

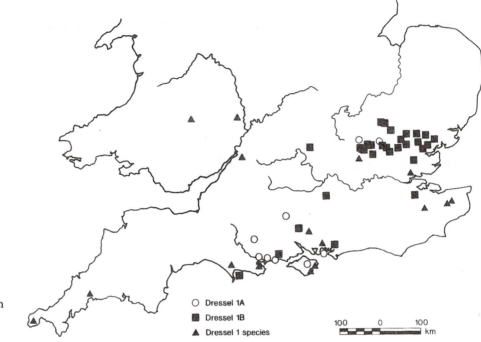

Map 6.1 Sites of Dressel 1 amphorae found in Britain. From Martin Millet, *The Romanization of Britain: An Essay in Archaeological Interpretation* (Cambridge: Cambridge University Press, 1990), map 9 (p. 32). Reproduced with permission of The Licensor through PLSclear.

could – but does not have to – have been such a comment. It turns out that Dressel 1 amphorae turn up in other graves in England (see Map 6.1), so it's best to ditch the idea that this one reflects an individual personality. But this issue does raise another one: who decided to put these objects in the grave, the deceased or his survivors? For that matter, did they belong to them or to his family or friends? The grave alone does not say.

With any source, it can be worth asking **What other evidence was found with the source?** This question can apply even to written evidence. For example, different texts can be bound together in one book; binding decisions can provide a clue as to what the person who made that decision thought was important about those texts and so put them together. But the question of context, the spatial relationship between an object and other material evidence, is especially likely to be important with archaeological sources. This discussion has already explored this aspect of the amphora: it was found in a grave with other high-status items, indicating a high-status individual. A closer look is, however, helpful. Some of the items were andirons, pig bones, remains of more bones in a cauldron, and bronze (and so valuable) dishes. Perhaps there had been a feast to send off the dead man, which would provide a different context for an amphora of wine. There were also two wooden buckets. (The wood disintegrated on excavation, but the metal fittings survived.) Written sources indicate the Romans customarily mixed their wine with water; perhaps that was what the buckets were for, strengthening the conclusion that the amphora was there as part of a ritual feast rather than as evidence that Roman culture was a status symbol.

Written sources and art seem to be the easiest path into the heads of people in the past. Sherds seem less promising, better for recovering brute and important material facts like trade contacts than for recovering tender attitudes and feelings. And perhaps they are. But sources – material as well as written – can always surprise.

PART III: SECONDARY SOURCES

chapter seven

Historians Presenting Original Research: Monographs and Articles

Historians draw their conclusions from primary sources. They make those conclusions available to readers in secondary sources, most typically in monographs, articles, and book chapters. A monograph is a book on a fairly narrow subject in which a historian presents new conclusions. Research articles are not found in newspapers or magazines, but in scholarly journals, aimed primarily at professional historians. They can also be found in focused scholarly books to which each researcher contributes a chapter, in which case the article is sometimes called a "book chapter." One characteristic of all these forms of original research is the heavy use of citations, either endnotes or footnotes. If the history you are reading does not bristle with notes, it is probably some other kind of secondary source (for some of these, see chapter 8). Although monographs usually have much more elaborate arguments than articles and are usually wider in scope, their structures are similar, so in discussing monographs I will also be covering articles. The same strategies and questions apply to both.

Typically, monographs have an overarching conclusion, or thesis, which the rest of the discussion is written to support. Articles have a similar structure. Your first mission, then, is to answer the question **What is the thesis?** and try to identify the author's own statement of it. But you should also be sure to express the thesis in your own words. Doing so is a way of making sure you understand it. Be likewise on the lookout for subordinate theses.

You should notice that a *thesis* is different from a *topic*. The topic is the subject – what the historian is talking about; the thesis is what the historian is trying to prove about the topic. If you are having trouble telling the difference, try to put what you think is the thesis in a form that completes the sentence "I will attempt to prove that...." If you can do this successfully, you have something that might be a thesis. If you cannot, you do not. Asking **What is the topic?** is worthwhile, but this is not the same as identifying the thesis. Consider, for example, "city cleaning in the Middle Ages." That is a topic and not a thesis. A thesis would be something like "Royal government in the Middle Ages mandated that city streets be kept clear of dung heaps because of a concern for traffic flow rather than public health."

Just because historians do their research in primary sources does not mean that secondary sources make no appearance in their monographs and articles. Authors of such works usually do their research in response not only to their reading of the primary sources, but to what other historians have said about the topic: to modify, strengthen, or reject the conclusions of earlier historians. In this way, historical research is usually part of an ongoing conversation among historians. Most history writers will indeed explain what previous historians have said about the topic or problem – something called the "historiography."[1] And understanding the historiography can help one understand the significance of the thesis under consideration. Thus, you will probably need to ask **How does the work respond to the historiography?** You will also need to ask **What is the overall argument in support of the thesis?** Moreover, historians will often draw on secondary sources simply as background or supplemental information or rely on the conclusions of secondary sources for a narrower point.

What is the best way to identify a historian's thesis? The first chapter or introduction is a natural place to look: historians often start out saying what the book seeks to prove and then use the rest of the book to do so. That first chapter will often include the broadest discussion of historiography, but you should also read the last chapter right after the first. Some historians will put their grand conclusion there rather than at the start. Reading a monograph is not like reading a murder mystery; it's not cheating to skip to the end. Now that you have read the first and last chapters, read the whole book from cover to cover, identifying what argument and evidence are deployed to support the thesis (or possibly theses). As you read each chapter, start by reading the first and last three or so paragraphs and then read the whole chapter through. Each chapter is likely to have a kind of chapter thesis that supports the book's thesis; you want to identify what that is. Try to write in your own words a sentence or two stating what each chapter is trying to show. (For an article, look to see if it is divided into sections and, if so, start with the first and last – or just the first few and last few paragraphs.)

Consider an excerpt from the first pages of the monograph *Out of Love for My Kin: Aristocratic Family Life in the Lands of the Loire, 1000–1200*, by Amy Livingstone.[2] In

---

1 "Historiography" can have a narrower or wider sense. The broadest meaning is the history of history as a field of study or research; the narrower sense is the history of what historians have said about a particular topic or issue. I am using the term in the narrower sense here.

2 Ithaca: Cornell University Press, 2010, 1–4.

this case, the subtitle indicates Livingstone's topic: aristocratic families of the Loire river valley, 1000–1200. But what is Livingstone's thesis, and what can one learn from her book about how a monograph is structured?

In the year 1102, records tell us, Adelina and Walter Minter and their children rode across the town of Chartres, passing under the shadow of the cathedral and traveling east through the winding streets and alleys of the market district of St. Père. Upon arriving at the monastery, they proceeded to the chapter house, where they arranged to give property to the brothers.

During their long marriage, Walter and Adelina had added to their joint inheritances by purchasing extensive properties, including fiefs, vineyards, land, houses, mills, and wine presses, thus giving them the means to make not only their original donation in 1102 to St. Père but also several more later on. After Walter died, Adelina and her six children continued working together to make profits from the original properties and to acquire additional wealth. As the children matured and eventually left the family home, each received a portion of the patrimony as well as what had been added to the family coffers. Three of Adelina and Walter's children married, two joined religious orders, and one son remained a bachelor. Once the earthly affairs of her family were settled, Adelina turned to the care of souls. She made a third donation to St. Père, this time to benefit her immortal soul and Walter's. This generous benefaction was made with her children's assent, which they gave of their own free will, and in the presence of the bishop and other powerful men in the region.

The experience of the Minter family and the details of these property arrangements give us important information about the family life of medieval elites. The grant of 1102 shows that Adelina was her husband's partner in making the transaction. The document's use of plural verbs makes the point that Adelina and Walter possessed and acquired the properties together and donated them together. Under the widow Adelina's watchful eye, the Minter family managed its property as a group, with each child having a share in the family resources. They cooperated in deciding which property would be used to endow those siblings who entered the church and they all agreed upon which properties would be used to commemorate their father and benefit their parents' souls. In short, we are left with the distinct impression that Adelina and Walter valued all their children, that each child enjoyed a portion of the family holdings, that the family took care in arranging the future of the family. That is, the Minters acted as many modern Western families do.

In this book, I will argue that the Minter family organization represents the norm rather than the exception among the aristocratic families of the lands of the Loire. I posit that an ethos of inclusivity lay at the center of aristocratic family life,

---

Historians often, although not always, begin with an anecdote or example that illustrates their thesis or the problem they want to address. Do not be thrown by this. Livingstone's thesis is not about the Minter family only.

This adds some human interest to the discussion but, as you will see, does not particularly pertain to Livingstone's thesis or argument. As you read, you will need to identify what details are important to the argument and what, like these, are not.

Here, Livingstone draws some specific conclusions from the Minters's property transactions but does not state a thesis for the book. She is setting up that thesis, however.

What is the thesis? Aha! Here Livingstone states a thesis, which can be rendered thus: Noble families in the Loire ca. 1000–1200 were concerned about all their members and women were partners of their husbands. The phrase "In this book, I will argue" helps clue you into this. (Not all historians are as considerate.) Note that the Minters appear here as just an example.

What is the thesis? Here Livingstone states her thesis more abstractly.

meaning that medieval aristocratic families cared about their members. As a consequence, these families put in place strategies, practices, and behaviors aimed at including a range of relatives in family life and providing for them. Indeed, this care – and in some cases outright affection – for family members is recorded in the documents themselves, as many a nobleman and woman made pious benefaction "out of love for my kin." Inclusivity was at play in aristocratic family dynamics in three significant ways.

First, medieval elites conceptualized their family broadly and did not give primacy to one line of descent. As is evident in the Minter family, both maternal and paternal kin were important and recognized, thus making aristocratic families collateral.[3] Inclusivity is also apparent in aristocrats' recognition of a wide range of kin and in the ways that medieval elite interacted with their kin throughout their lives. Second, far from adhering to one monolithic form of family structure or inheritance, the aristocracy of the Loire region implemented a variety of practices.... Third, the many roles that women played as influential members of their family demonstrate that they were not excluded from family decisions or made powerless by a system that invested authority solely in men....

In arguing that the private life of the nobility rested upon an ethos of inclusivity I challenge an older model that asserts that aristocrats implemented a family dynamic aimed at supporting only the line of the eldest son to the exclusion, and detriment, of other kin. Such a family structure was adopted in the eleventh century, so this model asserts, and represented a departure from previous practice as family dynamics shifted from inclusion to exclusion.[4] Yet, as I will argue in the pages to

---

What is the overall argument? Here it is, in three parts. These could be described as three sub-theses. Put them in your own words.

How does the work respond to the historiography? Here is a brief description of the historiography that Livingstone argues against.

Here Livingstone produces a kind of secondary thesis – that family structure in her study period (1000–1200) did not change very much from what it had been before.

This note is an example of the "discursive note": a note that discusses something that would not fit easily in the main text, and so a note that does not simply cite sources. It alone is a good sign that you should read the notes, not just the text, even if you do not plan to follow up by looking at sources.

---

3 [Livingstone's note:] A word about terminology and kinship patterns. *Patrilineage* represents a family configuration that has preference for the male line, particularly that of the firstborn son, over all others. *Cognatic kinship* refers to a kinship system that recognizes both the maternal and paternal lines.... Perhaps not surprisingly, kinship patterns shape inheritance practices. *Primogeniture*, or the inheritance by the firstborn son, often (but not always) accompanies a patrilineal-kinship organization. Partible, impartible, and shared all refer to inheritance strategies. *Partible* means that all children receive a share of family holdings. *Impartible* is the opposite, where inheritance is not split among heirs and is often, although not always, associated with patrilineage. Much in the way that primogeniture and patrilineage usually go together, so too cognatic kinship often appears in families practicing partible inheritance.

4 [Livingstone's note:] Georges Duby, while the most recognized proponent of this model, actually based his vision of aristocratic family life on the work of Karl Schmid. See Duby, *Medieval Marriage*; *The Knight the Lady and the Priest*; the essays collected in *The Chivalrous Society* and *Love and Marriage in the Middle Ages*; "Women and Power"; "Communal Living"; Duby and Braunstein, "Solitude"; Schmid, "Zur Problematik von Familie, Sippe und Geschlect, Haus und Dynastie beim mittelalterlichen Adel"; and "The Structure of the Nobility in the Earlier Middle Ages." For a recent analysis of the intersection of French and German scholarship, see Bernhard Jussen, "Famille et parenté."

come, the family practices of the twelfth-century Minters and their contemporaries did not differ significantly from those of their predecessors. An underlying theme of this book is that there was no fundamental shift in family structure during the period under examination, the eleventh through twelfth centuries.[5] Although families adjusted their inheritance patterns over time, there was not a mass abandonment of one system of inheritance or family structure for another.... While elegant in its simplicity, a model of patrilineage, primogeniture, and patriarchy does not accurately describe the family experience of the aristocracy of the lands of Loire.

Livingstone's theses appear to be that noble families in the Loire valley ca. 1000–1200 did not think of their families narrowly along male lines of descent, but instead included all family members. Wives were partners of their husbands, not simply subordinate. In all this, one can see continuity, not change, from the period before.

I cannot reproduce the whole of Livingstone's book here. But a look at the titles and subtitles of her chapters can you give a further idea of its contents. I should note that Livingstone's use of subchapter titles is especially extensive and explicit. She has an early subchapter on her primary sources, describing what kinds of sources are available to investigate aristocratic families and why her book will in particular stress charters (records of property transactions) as evidence. She notes that one reason she relies heavily on charters as sources rather than literature is that she is more concerned with actual people than the sort of general ideas about families one might recover from, say, literary sources.[6] Such a discussion of sources in general is not unusual. Her introduction also includes a chapter-by-chapter summary of the book. Not all historians provide this, but pay special attention when one does. Like many, although not all, monographs, Livingstone's provides a background chapter, explaining certain features of society and geography in the Loire valley in her period; such reading will be necessary for many readers in order to follow the later discussion, but it will be the later discussion that will be central to the book, not this sort of background information.

Your mission in reading the body of the book will be to assess how well or badly the historian uses evidence to support conclusions. One aspect of this is to ask the

> Here Livingstone restates the historiography she rejects, and in doing so, she makes more precise what is being rejected. She hinted at some of this in the previous paragraph too.

---

5 [Livingstone's note:] Given the significant political, economic, and cultural differences between the early and central Middle Ages, historians have assumed that family structure and inheritance must also differ radically between these two eras. Yet scholars have more recently come to recognize the continuities between these two time periods. See Jane Martindale, "The French Aristocracy in the Early Middle Ages: A Reappraisal"; Constance B. Bouchard, "The Origins of the French Nobility: A Reassessment"; Dominique Barthélemy, "La mutation féodale a-t-elle eu lieu?"; Jeffrey A. Bowman, *Shifting Landmarks*; and Richard E. Sullivan, "The Carolingian Age." The scholarship on the medieval family has been affected by this larger trend in medieval historiography.

6 Livingstone, 3.

> Livingstone is noting how her conclusions harmonize with those of other scholars working in her period, although not on her topic.

following questions: **Does the historian deal with evidence that undermines the thesis or at least appears to?** *If so, how well or badly?* Livingstone provides an example of a historian dealing with such countervailing evidence here:[7]

> In spite of such interactions [in which mothers influenced or tried to influence the decisions of their adult sons] the role of mothers has often been overlooked. Part of the reason for this may lay with the extant charters themselves, which can obscure the activities of women in aristocratic society. Take, for example, two charters recording a donation made by the Legedoctus family. "Let it be known by all posterity that Helvisa Legedocta gave to St. Martin the tithes from the church of St John of Chamars, except [those] from bread and wine, and three arpents of land in the cemetary. To this her son Robert [and many clerics and her other children] consented."[8] The transaction took place in Helvisa's house and her lord, the viscount of Châteaudun, approved the transfer. Yet a later episcopal confirmation recorded the act differently. Bishop Ivo confirmed that the tithes pertaining to the church known as St John of Chamars were given by Robert Legedoctus and his mother Helvisa.[9] The episcopal document clearly casts the transaction in a different light from the original grant, relegating Helvisa to the role of supporting character as opposed to her true role in the gift as main actor. For whatever reason, the scribe (or the bishop himself) chose to make Robert the donor. It is possible that other documents suffered a similar redaction and may account for, or certainly contribute to, a skewed model of women's experience as one of oppression or powerlessness.[10]

In other words, yes, there are lots of charters in which women are not the decision makers – which cuts against Livingstone's argument about the authority of noblewomen – but since there was a practice to make charters that downplayed the role mothers were really playing, women could really have been playing a larger role in such transactions than the mass of charters indicates. Livingstone thus acts to defang a potential argument against her.

Citations of manuscript sources can be rather cryptic for those who do not know that archive.

Note how Livingstone reinforces her argument by pointing to other scholars who've found similar practices in other parts of medieval France. This is another use of secondary sources in a monograph.

7 Livingstone, 47–8. The insertions into quotations in this passage are Livingstone's.

8 [Livingstone's note:] AD Eure-et-Loire, H 2268. Helvisa's other children also consented to the grant, although the section confirming their approval comes at the bottom of the charter. This might suggest that Robert had some special claim to the property in question. Perhaps it was to be his inheritance. Perhaps he was the eldest child – although none of the acts designate him so. Or perhaps it was a scribal convenience.

9 [Livingstone's note:] AD Eure-et-Loire, H 2268.

10 [Livingstone's note:] Scholars working on regions of medieval France have detected similar scribal practices that ultimately result in an underreporting of women in the charters. See Elisabeth Carpentier, "La place des femmes dans la plus anciennes chartes poitevins"; and Jean Gay, "Remarques sur l'évolution de la pratique contractuelle en Champagne méridionale (XIIe-XIXe siècle)."

When you read, subject the arguments and the evidence used to support them to the "worst-enemy test." Ask yourself: **How strong is the evidence and the argument from that evidence?** *In other words, if you were this historian's worst enemy, how might you attack, in a specific way, the historian's evidence and reasoning from that evidence?* In this case, you might conclude that Livingstone's evidence of a transaction rewritten in order to reduce a mother's role indicates that the larger culture did not approve of women having such authority. Mothers who did what Helvisa Legedocta in the first charter did were thus exceptional – the very reverse of what Livingstone wants to show. In reply, Livingstone might point out that her goal – noted above – is to "reconstruct the lives of actual individuals,"[11] so talking about medieval models or expectations regarding behavior is beside the point. On the other hand, could not such models or expectations be presumed to have affected actual behavior? This imaginary discussion between you and Livingstone could go further, but I have illustrated my point. The goal of being a devil's advocate here is not to be an ass; the goal is to come to a reasoned conclusion as to whether to believe those arguments. By testing what you read in this way, you are positioned to decide whether you know the truth of what you read.

Notice how the previous paragraph's challenge to Livingstone did not rely on any knowledge of aristocratic family life in the Middle Ages other than what is presented by Livingstone herself. This shows that you do not need to know about the subject matter of a work of history in order to assess that work's use of evidence. True, an expert on the Middle Ages might have other questions to put to Livingstone. But you do not have to be an expert to decide for yourself whether a historian is persuasive. You need to read and think carefully.

Here is a somewhat different example of a monograph: excerpts from the first chapter of *The Goddess and the Nation: Mapping Mother India* by Sumathi Ramaswamy.[12] It is rather less direct than Livingstone, a characteristic it shares with many monographs.

> In the closing decades of the nineteenth century in a land already thronging with all manner of gods and goddesses there surfaced a novel deity of nation and country who at some moments in the subsequent years seemed to tower over them all. Invoked in English as "Mother India," and most usually in various Indian languages as "Bhahat Mata" (literally "India Mother"), she was over time imagined as the substantial embodiment of national territory – its inviolable essence, its shining beacon of hope and liberation – and also as a powerful rallying symbol in its long

11 Livingstone, 3.
12 Durham: Duke University Press, 2010, 1–3, 6–7.

hard struggle for independence from the modern world's largest empire.[13] Over the next half century and more, as the subcontinent itself was transformed from Britain's most important colony into the free states of India and Pakistan, she gathered together in common celebration and devotion large sections of the region's vast population fissured by caste, language, ethnicity, and local and regional sentiments even as she came to be perceived as escalating the irrevocable rupture catastrophically developing between its two dominant religious communities, Hindu and Muslim.[14] This book is about this new and unusual mother/goddess and her complicated entanglement in the Indian nation's attempts to create for itself a visible and tangible form over the course of a century that began in the 1880s. Specifically, in these pages I analyze the myriad ways in which Mother India has been visualized in painting, print, poster art, and pictures, with a view toward developing a key proposition. Despite the venerable antiquity in which Bharat Mata has been presented to her (Indian) beholders, she is the tangled product of charged encounters between the new and the old and of a fraught and conflicted modernity that is India's late colonial

---

13 [Ramaswamy's note:] The Sanskrit word *Bharata* (which combines with *mata*, a generic Indo-Aryan term for mother, to form the compound *Bharat Mata*) has a long and complicated history that can be traced to at least the first millennium BCE as the name used to designate the territorial space we now refer to as India, the people who lived in a part of this land, and the ideal king who ruled over them. For an important discussion of how this term was recuperated in late colonial India, see Goswami 2004, esp. chapter 6. The Constitution of India (which went into effect on January 26, 1950) specifically identifies the country as Bharat, thereby disclosing the Sanskritic, Aryan, and Hindu moorings of this democratic republic that in 1976 after a critical amendment also declared itself to be "secular" and "socialist." See also my discussion in chapter 4, n. 17.

14 [Ramaswamy's note:] In contrast with the term *Muslim*, the word *Hindu* (and the religion associated with it, Hinduism, an appellation largely of nineteenth-century provenance) is notoriously difficult to define. Given the territorial focus of my work, it is worth noting that the term Hindu is the ancient Persian variant of the Sanskrit name Sindhu, which refers to the Indus river and is in turn the inspiration for the Greek name India. From the sixth century BCE the plural form of *Hindu* identifies the people of the region ("the Indus people"). Importantly, with the arrival of Islam in the subcontinent the term *Hindu* came to be used first as an ethnic designation for non-Muslim people in Persian sources from the late first millennium CE, regardless of their differing belief systems. From the eleventh century, but especially after a series of Mongol invasions in the thirteenth century, the term *Hindu* comes to take on an explicit religious connotation in distinction from *Muslim* in Arabic and Persian narratives of the region. Although no single tenet or practice is universally shared across the subcontinent by those who call themselves Hindu, the recognition of the authority of the Vedas, a conviction about reincarnation and the doctrine of karma, and a social system rooted in caste-based distinctions are diagnostic elements. More pertinently for this work, the wide acceptance of a multiplicity of deities, a recognition that virtually anyone or anything has divine potential, a proclivity toward bestowing form (particularly anthropomorphic form) on the divine, and the establishment of ritual programs to worship such embodied forms distinguish the Hindu from the Muslim in theological as well as social terms over the course of the twentieth century.

Here Ramaswamy states the topic.

This cues the thesis. It's coming. Calling it "a key proposition" is the kind of understatement historians frequently make regarding their theses.

Here we have a thesis statement. Again, put it in your own words – for example, "Indians liked to think of the image of Mother India as old. But it was really a product of tradition interacting with the new."

This is, in a sense, "pure background." But it does lend a kind of indirect support to Ramaswamy's argument that Mother India helped solidify the very notion of India and India as a Hindu nation.

As Ramaswamy notes, this background information is more pertinent to her argument. This is because Mother India draws on this Hindu tendency to depict gods and goddesses in human form.

and postcolonial experience of history.[15] Mother India's hesitant novelty and ambiguous modernity only becomes apparent, however, if we consider her diverse pictorial appearances, for much of the abundant poetry and prose utterances on the goddess contrarily clothe her in the archaic and root her in an immemorial past.

This pictorial history of Mother India seeks to understand why a nation striving to be secular, diverse, and modern would also resort to the timeworn figure of a Hindu goddess in its yearning for form.[16] What is at stake in drawing such a tendentious female form to picture a sovereign national territory that has also sought to project itself as a culturally and religiously plural body politic? This study also explores how the divinized Mother India becomes a focal point for many of the developing nation's contentious debates between authenticity and imitation, between tradition and modernity and religion and science, and between being essentially Hindu but aspiring simultaneously to secularity and pluralism, to name the most urgent. How do such struggles leave their traces on this embattled embodiment of the nation? Not least, against the ingrained anti-visualism of the social sciences, in this book I insist that pictures, too, have stories to show and arguments to manifest, and that images are not just illustrative and reflective but also constitutive and world-making rather than world-mirroring.[17] How do such visual displays and pictorial revelations relate to verbal histories and prosaic narratives? What are the points of convergences, and as important, how do we account

As will be spelled out subsequently, Ramaswamy's prime evidence is visual. Here she indicates that this kind of evidence supports conclusions different from that of the (written) sources used by other historians so far for this topic.

Ramaswamy's thesis says the image of Mother India combined the new and the old. This is the old element: a Hindu (style) goddess.

This appears to be a kind of secondary thesis: that images of Mother India reveal or reflect conflicts in India over these issues.

Sometimes historians use a new approach – a methodology – and a point they want to make is the value of that methodology. Ramaswamy's approach is that images can shape the world rather than just reflect it. The book is also an argument for the value of this idea.

---

15 [Ramaswamy's note:] There is a vast and rich literature on the idea of modernity, which when addressed in a note, runs the risk of caricature. My normative understanding follows from what Jürgen Habermas (1983) called the Enlightenment project of modernity with its emphasis on the accumulation of knowledge for the purpose of human emancipation and the enrichment of daily life; the scientific domination of nature; the autonomy of art; and the development of rational forms of social and political organization and rational modes of thought that seek to liberate the individual from myth, religion, and superstition. Much of the past two decades of postcolonial scholarship on Europe's colonies, India included, have [sic] been dedicated to debating the extent to which such processes devolved in places and societies far away from the metropole, and to foregrounding the violence wrought in the name of modernization by Europe over the rest of the world (see, in this regard, Bhabha 1994; Chakrabarty 2000; Cohn 1996; and Nandy 2001). Also important for my argument are the insights of Martin Heidegger (1997, 134) who draws attention to novel forms of representation ushered in by modernity that result in "the conquest of the world as picture" so that the world appears to us as framed or frameable. The scientific map form is a critical example of such processes, and I address this issue further in the epilogue.

16 [Ramaswamy's note:] I am adapting here from Brennan (1990) who considers how the novel bestows form on the nation, and from Biggs (1999) who demonstrates how cartography bestowed geographic form on the territorial state in early modern Europe.

17 [Ramaswamy's note:] I have been influenced by my reading of scholars like James Elkins, Martin Jay, W.J.T. Mitchell, and especially Barbara Stafford (1995), who offers a powerful set of arguments against the "degradation of images" and "entrenched antivisualism" in post-Enlightenment thought.

Here is another use of secondary sources: to get inspiration for questions to ask or arguments to make from studies of other times and places.

Historians sometimes explicitly draw on social, cultural, or other theory.

for the differences? This, then, is a book about pictorial ways of learning the nation and visually coming to know it and live with it – and ultimately to die for it.[18]

Although she is not quite as explicit about it as Livingstone on the Minters, Ramaswamy is using this picture as an illustrative example of her thesis.

> It is fitting to begin this pictorial history in 1997 with a triptych published in one of the country's leading English-language dailies, the *Times of India*, to commemorate the fiftieth anniversary of Indian independence from colonial rule on August 15, 1947. In the middle panel of this triptych, as the accompanying text states, the "contours of our great country transform into the image of Mother India sprinkling Ganga [Ganges] water from one hand, the other releasing the bird of freedom, Ganesha[19] perched on her arm like Bhujpal [the strong armed] (figure 1) [figure 7.1 in this book].

As the sun rises over the jagged Himalayan peaks alongside a crescent moon, Mother India appears as a youthful woman whose torso and limbs are playfully arranged to approximate an outline map of India....

Given Ramaswamy's stress on the power of images, this description is noteworthy.

I have chosen to begin this pictorial history of Mother India with these works by Maqbool Fida Husain[20] (b. 1915) because they demonstrate that even one of the most famous of India's artists occupying the very pinnacle of its national and international circuit of fine art felt persuaded to visualize Indian national territory by turning to the female form – highly stylized though it may appear on his canvasses....[21] Most saliently ... for a key proposition of this book, in Husain's pictures of Bharat Mata her body is conspicuously carto-graphed to approximate the scientifically shaped map of India, a product of recent colonial history.[22] In turn, the map of India – that

A heads-up that what follows will be important for her thesis.

Again, inspiration from studies of other times and places: Landes's work cited here is on the French Revolution.

---

18 [Ramaswamy's note:] In asking such questions I am adapting from many recent works that have contributed to the new visual or pictorial turn in cultural history (in particular Landes 2001 and Pinney 2004). My larger understanding of colonial Indian visual history has also been informed by the exemplary analyses found in Freitag 2001; Guha-Thakurta 1992, 2004; Jain 2007; and Mitter 1994.

19 An elephant-headed god, one of the most important of the Hindu gods.

20 The first of these was just discussed in this excerpt.

21 [Ramaswamy's note:] In spite or perhaps because of the many controversies in which the artist is embroiled, including the recent one surrounding his nude Bharat Mata, his admirers, among them the country's leading artists and writers, launched a campaign to persuade the Government of India to bestow upon him the nation's highest civilian honor, the Bharat Ratna. In the words of the nominating petition, Husain's "life and work are beginning to serve as an allegory for the changing modalities of the secular in modern India – and the challenges that the narrative of the nation holds for many of us." "Letter to the President of India," in *Maqbool Fida Husain* 2008, 122.

22 [Ramaswamy's note:] Following from an understanding of cartography as a set of practices and techniques through which spatial knowledge is produced through the visual technology of the map (Biggs 1999), I use the neologism "carto-graphed" to draw attention to the yoking together of the human or divine body and cartographic products like maps and globes to produce a particular kind of spatial knowledge. In this study, a carto-graphed body is one that is inscribed in the form of a map, or drawn to accommodate, outline, or be attached to the map form of a country.

proud creation of a self-consciously rational and modern science – is deeply gendered and divinized through its occupation by the figure of a Hindu goddess, its cartographic space filled up with her anthropomorphic presence....[23]

Maqbool Fida Husain is one among a long line of artists and illustrators who since the early years of the twentieth century have felt persuaded to visualize India as a carto-graphed mother/goddess.[24]

Evidently, Ramaswamy's thesis is that the combination of a figure modeled on Hindu goddesses with maps of India in the depiction of Mother India indicates that Mother India was a fusion of traditional and modern, scientific elements. One point is worth noting: although Ramaswamy states her thesis early on, she does not spell it out in terms of the union of the goddess figure and the map of India, and which is old and which is new, in the first section of the book. The various elements of the thesis are a bit dispersed. You, the attentive reader, need to put them together.

Historians often write in response to the historiography. They sometimes also write in some way in response to their own time. Such connections can usually be found only by reading between the lines; historians tend not to spell them out or are even themselves unaware of them. Consider Livingstone's book: her women are active agents rather than subordinate to

Figure 7.1 Maqbool Fida Husain, Center Panel of *50 Years of Emerging India*: a triptych illustration for *The Times of India* (Bombay), Special Supplement, August 15, 1997.

Note that maps are thus scientific and modern; here, then, is a new element in the image of Mother India, which is thus fused with the old (a Hindu goddess), affirming Ramaswamy's thesis. Note that so far this important element of her thesis appears in a note. It will appear in the text only later.

Here Ramaswamy provides a brief historiography of her specific topic, the image of Mother India. Notably, she points out that there is no monograph dedicated to the subject – so, hers is the first – and that no one has thoroughly examined the role maps play in the image – so, she has something new to add.

---

23 [Ramaswamy's note:] Throughout this study I subscribe to a revisionist understanding of maps as "graphic representations that facilitate a spatial understanding of things, concepts, conditions, processes or events in the modern world ... [.] Maps are the artifacts that store, communicate, and promote spatial understanding" (Harley and Woodward 1987, xvi). My understanding of scientific or cartographic maps as mathematizing the world is also informed by J. Brian Harley's brilliant work in *The New Nature of Maps* (2001), by the writings of several postmodern historians of cartography and geography (see Cosgrove 2001, 2005; Pickles 2004) and Bruno Latour's many meditations on mediation (see Latour 1986, 1988, 1990, 1998).

24 [Ramaswamy's note:] There is no scholarly monograph on Mother India despite her salience, but see Bagchi 1990; Bannerjee 2002; Bose 1997; Brosius 2005; Chowdhury 1998; Goswami 2004; Gupta 2002; Kaur 2003; McKean 1996; Sarkar 2001, 2006; and Sen 2002 for important discussions about her emergence in Bengal in the late 1860s, her growing popularity as a nationalist symbol in the early years of the twentieth century, the escalating anxieties among some over her role in alienating Muslim citizens, and her recent resurgence in the cultural politics of Hindi nationalism. Her visualization is discussed in Guha-Thakurta 1992; Jha 2004; Mitter 1994; Sen 2002; Uberoi 1990, 2003; Sinha 2006; and especially Neumayer and Schelberger 2008. Virtually no one has elaborated on the critical role played by the map of India in Mother India's iconography, but for some important beginnings in this direction, see the work of the anthropologist Christiane Brosius (1997; 2005, ch. 4; 2006) and the art historian Geeti Sen (2002). My scholarship in these pages and in other essays builds on this body of work (see Ramaswamy 2001, 2002, 2003).

men. One could argue that she is thus responding to the feminism of her (that is, our) time. But one should be careful of such arguments. After all, had she argued that women were oppressed by men, *that* also could be ascribed to feminist influence. Perhaps it would be safer to say that the very fact that she is interested in whether women had autonomy is a response to the feminist movement. In any case, she herself does not draw a connection between feminism and her book.

It is easier to argue that current concerns inform Ramaswamy's account. She discusses the Hindu nationalism of her (and our) own time, which defines Indian nationhood in terms of Hinduism (thus excluding non-Hindus, particularly Muslims). Indeed, that Hindu nationalism may have inspired her to investigate this topic. Although she does not say so, her discussion cuts against nationalist accounts of India as a nation that is ancient: she sees Mother India as a modern figure, not an ancient one. What is clear is that one should ask of any work of history: **Does the work reflect the time in which it was written?** *If so, does this introduce a bias that affects the argument?* Even if the answer to the first question is yes, the answer to the second question may be yes or no. That means you have to do what you have to do anyway: consider the historian's use of evidence carefully.

chapter eight

Textbooks, Popular History, and Secondary Sources Online

8.1 Textbooks

History textbooks typically seek not to reveal new discoveries, but to summarize the current state of knowledge for students. In this sense, they are very different from the monographs and articles discussed in the last chapter. Another difference is that textbooks often simply try to convey information rather than make arguments backed by evidence. (There are certainly exceptions to this, and you should be on the lookout for them.) Those tendencies can also make textbooks simply look different from other kinds of historical writing. Where monographs are clotted with citations, textbooks cite sources only occasionally if at all, and their bibliographies serve more as directions to further reading than as a list of primary sources on which the author relies and secondary sources to which the author responds. Moreover, textbooks often include pictures supplied often more to enliven the text than to serve as evidence for an author's claims. Insertions – bits of text set off from the rest by a box – are common. The more introductory the textbook, the more likely it is to have these features.

Textbooks can be harder to read than monographs. On the one hand, textbooks are less technical and their authors may try harder to be readable. On the other hand, monographs have a natural structure: discussion of how historians have dealt with a historical question and a thesis in response to that question, sometimes followed by a discussion of the chief primary sources for the topic, with the rest of the discussion (more or less) used to marshal evidence and argument to support that thesis. Because textbooks do often aim at broad coverage and summary, their structure can be less obvious. Moreover, the attempt to summarize a lot in a small space can produce a certain vagueness; it's possible to read some textbooks and come away with a few conclusions that are so general that they seem mushy. (Any textbook writer is in danger of writing the sentence "[Insert name of any society] had a rich and vibrant culture." Was there ever any culture that could not be described in these terms?) There are, however, some ways of approaching textbook reading to avoid these problems:

- As with a monograph, read the start and end of any chapter first. If the author makes larger points, they will likely appear there.
- Pay attention to titles of chapters and subchapters.
- First check the start and end of the chapter for any study questions. Such questions can be the author's way of directing you to especially important issues.
- Pay special attention to pictures and even maps and their captions. While such material can be there just to make the book more fun, it can be used to provide examples of more general statements in the text.
- If the author provides a vocabulary list, pay attention to those terms in the text. The author thinks they are important.
- Be prepared to read the text (at least) twice. Do so once before class; the greater familiarity with the subject will probably help you follow what is going on in class. Read it again after class; in class, your instructor may highlight certain important issues, putting you in a better position to pick up on those matters when you reread the text. Or ask your instructor when to read.
- Take notes as you go, either in the margin of the book or on a separate paper. You are much more likely to remember what you read if you do so. Highlighting with a marker or underlining is less likely to have this effect.

One can see how to apply these approaches when reading the first few pages and the last page of chapter 14 of a commonly used introductory textbook: Albert Craig et al., *The Heritage of World Civilizations*.[1] The chapter's topic is clear from its title: "Africa ca. 1000–1700." Notice the absence of citations.

---

1 Ninth ed. (Upper Saddle River, NJ: Pearson Prentice-Hall, 2011), vol. 2, 401–4, 422.

- North Africa and Egypt

- The Spread of Islam South of the Sahara

- Sahelian Empires of the Western and Central Sudan

- The Eastern Sudan

- The Forestlands – Coastal West and Central Africa

- East Africa

- Southern Africa

THE HISTORY OF AFRICA IN THE FIRST HALF OF THE second millennium C.E. varied considerably in different regions. Many parts of Africa had substantial interactions with the Islamic and European worlds; others were engaged in trade and cultural exchanges within the continent.

The Atlantic slave trade affected almost all of Africa between the fifteenth and nineteenth centuries and is treated in Chapter 17. However, here we cannot overlook its importance in disrupting and reconfiguring African economies, social organization, and politics.

We begin with Africa above the equator, where Islam's influence increased and substantial kingdoms and empires flourished. Then we discuss West, East, central, and southern Africa and the effects of Arab-Islamic and then European influence in these regions.

The slave trade with the New World will mostly be dealt with elsewhere, but its effects on Africa will be dealt with in this chapter.

[Caption of photograph:][2] **The Great Mosque at Kilwa, ca. 1100 C.E.** The Swahili city of Kilwa, on the coast of present-day Tanzania, was likely founded by Muslim traders with strong links to the Indian Ocean world. The insides of its domes were lined with Chinese porcelain. Now in ruins, this large congregational mosque was probably in its day the largest fully enclosed structure in sub-Saharan Africa.

A reaffirmation that the chapter's organization will be geographical.

Once again, the authors say they will discuss relations between the Islamic world and Europe, on the one hand, and Africa on the other. Given the previous two paragraphs, it looks like this will be a major, perhaps the major, point of the chapter.

Conveniently, our authors start out with a list of chapter subheadings. Note that these are all geographical, so that is how the chapter will be organized. It would make sense at this point to find a map in the chapter and locate these various regions, perhaps even marking them.

So, different regions were different. Some interacted with outsiders: the Islamic world and/or Europe.

---

2 I have not included the maps or photographs that appear in this textbook. I have included the captions to the latter.

Global Perspective

Africa, 1000–1700

Long distance trade – the supply-and-demand-driven movement of goods, people, and cultural attitudes and practices – typically stimulates historical change. This was as true in Africa in the early second millennium as in the Americas, Europe, and Asia. Different African regions were oriented differently vis-à-vis trade routes and trading partners and consequently developed in markedly different ways in these centuries.

The North African coast and the Sahel lay amidst trading networks linking the Mediterranean world, the growing **Dar-al-Islam** ("House of Submission" – the Islamic realm), and the rich West African kingdoms. The East

African coast was integrated into the trading and cultural networks of the Indian Ocean basin and firmly engaged with the Islamic world. The rest of sub-Saharan Africa was culturally diverse; people here engaged in intra-African trade with cultures occupying different ecological niches. Africa is home to many societies with different histories, languages, religions, and cultures. In this it is

Here starts a pretty extended discussion set off from the main text. It turns out that it highlights important developments also treated, but with less emphasis, in the main text.

So trade was a – even *the* – major means by which Africans outside of North Africa interacted with the Islamic world.

North Africa and Egypt

As we saw in Chapter 12, Egypt and other North African societies played a central role in Islamic and Mediterranean history after 1000 C.E. From Tunisia to Egypt, Sunni religious and political leaders and their Shi'ite, especially Isma'ili, counterparts struggled for the minds of the masses. By the thirteenth century, however, the Shi'ites had become a small minority of the Muslims in Mediterranean Africa. In Egypt a Sunni revival confirmed the Sunni character of Egyptian religiosity and legal interpretation. In general, a feisty regionalism characterized states, city-states, and tribal groups north

of the Sahara and along the lower Nile. No single power controlled them for long. Regionalism persisted even after 1500, when most of North Africa came under the influence – and often, direct control – of the Ottoman Empire centered in Istanbul and felt the pressure of Ottoman-European naval rivalry.

By 1800 the nominally Ottoman domains from Egypt to Algeria were effectively independent. In

Here, the text supplies examples of the regionalism that meant Ottoman control over North Africa was nominal only.

So, despite official Ottoman control after 1500, North Africa was not politically united.

similar to, but much larger and more ethnically diverse than, Europe.

In Mediterranean Africa, the major new reality in these centuries was Ottoman imperial expansion into Egypt and the **Mahgreb**. Ottoman hegemony altered the political configuration of the Mediterranean. Merchants and missionaries carried Islam and Arabian culture across the Sahara from North Africa and the Middle East to western, central, and Nilotic Sudan (see Map 14-2 on page 409), where Muslim conversion played a growing social and political role, especially among ruling elites who profited most

Trade and Islam again!

Egypt, the Ottomans had established direct rule by defeating the Mamluks in 1517, but by the seventeenth and eighteenth centuries, power had passed to the Egyptian governors descended from the earlier Mamluks. These governors survived until the rise of Muhammed Ali in the wake of the French invasion of 1800 (see Chapter 26). The Mediterranean coastlands between Egypt and Morocco were officially Ottoman provinces, or regencies. By the 1700s, however, Algiers was a locally run principality with an economy based on piracy. Tripoli (in modern Libya) was ruled by a family of hereditary, effectively independent rulers, and Tunisia was virtually independent of its nominal Ottoman overlords.

Morocco, ruled by a succession of **Sharifs** (leaders claiming descent from the prophet's family) was the only North African sultanate to remain fully independent after 1700. The most important *Sharifian* dynasty was that of the Sa'dis (1554–1649). Morocco's independence was largely due to the uniting of its Arab and Berber populations after 1500 to oppose Portuguese and Spanish threats.

[Caption for photograph:] **The Great Mosque in Timbuktu.** This mud and wood building is typical of western Sudanese mosques. The distinctive tower of the mosque was a symbol of Islam, which came to places like Timbuktu in central and West Africa by overland trade routes.

So, the authors include a photograph of a mosque; that mosque itself serves as evidence of Islamic influence – or at least of Islamic presence south of the Sahara. Note that the authors say Timbuktu lay on a trade route, reinforcing the conclusion that Islam arrived via trade.

from brokering trade with the Islamic north. Islam provided a shared arena of expression for at least some of the social groups and classes over a vast area from Egypt to Senegambia. In Africa as elsewhere, new converts adapted Islam to local circumstances. Distinctively African Islamic forms resulted, faithful to basic Islamic tenets but differing from "classical" Arabo-Persian forms, especially in attitudes toward women and relationships between the sexes.

South of the Sahara, dynamic state-building and trade were principal motors of cultural change. In sub-Saharan Africa, except on the east coast and in the West African forests, older African traditions held sway, and there

was little or no Islamic presence beyond individual Muslims involved in trade. On the east coast, however, Islam influenced the development of Swahili culture and language, a unique blend of African, Indian, and

So, Islam, where adopted, was adjusted to local conditions.

Islam and trade again, although in some areas, Islamic influence was confined to trade.

And the caption above of the Great Mosque at Kilwa demonstrates this – note the mention of Chinese porcelain inside the domes and the reference to Muslim-facilitated trade with China here. Note also that the text does not refer to this mosque.

The Spread of Islam South of the Sahara

Islamic influence in sub-Saharan Africa began as early as the eighth century and by 1800 affected most of the Sudanic belt and East African coast as far south as modern Zimbabwe. Islam's spread was mostly peaceful, gradual, and partial. Conversion to Islam was rare beyond the ruling or commercial classes, and Islamic faith tended to co-exist or blend with indigenous traditions. Nevertheless, agents of Islam brought not only the Qur'an, new religious practices, and literate culture, but also commercial and political changes, which substantially affected subsequent history. Many innovations, from architecture and technology to intellectual life and administrative practice, depended on writing and literacy, two major bases for developing large-scale societies and cultures.

Again: Islam was spread through trade.

Comparison of the spread of Islam in West and central Africa with that in East Africa is instructive. In East Africa, Muslim traders moving down the coastline with the ancient monsoon trade routes had begun to "Islamize" ports and coastal regions even before 800 C.E. From the thirteenth century on, Islamic trading communities and city-states developed along the coast from Mogadishu to Kilwa. By contrast, in Western and central

So, Islamization south of the Sahara was rare beyond rulers and traders.

But the impact of Islam south of the Sahara was substantial, even without large-scale conversion to Islam. For the "large-scale societies and cultures" it made possible, see below.

Arabian traditions, and Muslim traders linked this region to India, China, and the Indies. In West Africa, Islamic states became important centers of Muslim culture and faith. Throughout sub-Saharan Africa, the spread of Islam occurred almost entirely by peaceful means.

Along the Atlantic and Indian Ocean coasts of Africa, the key fifteenth-century development was the shipboard arrival of traders and missionaries from Christian Europe. The strength of African societies and the biological dangers to Europeans in the African interior meant that most of Europeans' trade with the interior on both coasts remained for generations under African control. Well before Europeans reached the interior, however, the trade in slaves, weapons, and gold they fostered greatly altered African political and social structures both along the coasts and in regions untouched by outsiders. The European voyages of discovery of the 1400s and 1500s presaged Africa's involvement in a new, expanding and, by the 1700s, European-dominated global trading system. This system generally exploited rather than bolstered African development, as the Atlantic

slave trade (see Chapter 17) and the South African experience illustrate.

Focus Questions

■ Where in Africa was Islamic influence concentrated? How did Islam spread? What does this reveal about the relationship between commerce and cultural diffusion?

■ Why did different regions in Africa develop in different ways between 1000 and 1700?

So, here are some questions that can help you navigate the prior set-off content. It would not be a bad idea to reread the above discussion with these questions in mind. And be on the lookout for such questions before reading any section of the book.

European contact was important because of the impact of the European slave trade and Africa's integration into a larger world-trade network.

Africa, Islam was introduced into the Sudan by overland routes, primarily through traders from North Africa and the Nile valley. Berbers who, as early as the eighth century, plied the desert routes (see Chapter 5)[3] to trading towns such as Awdaghast on the edge of the Sahel were Islam's chief agents. From there Islam spread south to centers such as Kumbi Saleh, southeast across the Niger, and west into Senegambia. Another source of Islam's penetration into the central and western Sudan was migration from Egypt and the Nilotic Sudan. In particular, migrating Arab tribal groups in search of new land came west to settle in the central sub-Saharan Sahel....

---

3 The authors refer here to Chapter 5 of *The Heritage of World Civilizations*, not to chapter 5 of this book.

These conclusions pertain to the portion of the chapter included above. Did you read them first?

Summary

North Africa. From 1000 to 1700 in North Africa, the key new factor was the Ottoman Empire's expansion as far west as Morocco. But the development of independent regional rulers soon rendered Ottoman authority in North Africa largely nominal.

Empires of the Sudan. Several substantial states arose south of the Sahara: Ghana, Mali, Songhai, and Kanem. The ruling elites of these states converted to or were heavily influenced by Islam, although most of their populations practiced local religions. Much of these states' wealth was tied to their control of the trans-Saharan trade routes. Farther south, in the coastal forestlands of central Africa, another substantial kingdom arose in Benin, famous for its brass sculptures.

East Africa. On the east coast, Islam influenced the development of the distinctive Swahili culture and language, and Islamic traders linked the region to India and East Asia.

The Coming of the Europeans. The key development of the fifteenth century was the arrival of European traders, missionaries, and warships. The Portuguese and later Europeans came in search of commerce, Christian converts, and spheres of influence. Their arrival disrupted indigenous African culture and political relations and presaged Africa's involvement in and exploitation by a new, expanding global trading system dominated by Europeans.

Key terms

[Fifteen terms are listed, including those in **bold** in the excerpt above.]

Review Questions

To what extent can you answer these questions just from what you read?

1. Why did Islam succeed in sub-Saharan and East Africa? What role did warfare play? Trade?

2. What is the world historical significance of the empires in Ghana, Mali, and Songhai? Why was the control of the trans-Saharan trade crucial for these kingdoms? What was the importance of Islamic culture to them? Why did each empire break up?

3. What was the impact of the Portuguese on East Africa? on central Africa? How did the European coastal activities affect the interior?

4. How did the Portuguese and Dutch differ from or resemble the Arabs and other Muslims who came as outsiders to sub-Saharan Africa?

5. Discuss the diversity of Cape society in South Africa before 1700. Who were the Trekboers, and what was their conflict with the Khoikhoi? How was the basis for apartheid formed in this period?

Reading a textbook well can be crucial to succeeding in a class. When the textbook is important, it pays to tackle it with a plan.

8.2 Popular History

As the term implies, popular history aims to inform or simply entertain the general public. This fact explains why such histories generally look different on the page from monographs: no notes, or very few. Publishers are convinced that the public is afraid of footnotes or even endnotes. Moreover, popular histories often seek less to create new historical knowledge than to convey the research found in monographs and articles in a more readable way – citation of sources thus becomes less important. Popular histories also have more pictures than monographs and those pictures are more likely present to add color rather than serve as evidence for an argument. In these ways, popular histories are more like textbooks than monographs. Popular histories typically lack, however, the inserts common in introductory textbooks. Their authors work harder to write engaging prose; writers of monographs sometimes suspect that this means cutting corners when it comes to rigor. Sometimes writers of monographs are right about this; sometimes they are wrong. *Indeed, all of the above statements are generalizations*: there are exceptions.

A good example of a popular history is John Freely's *Inside the Seraglio: Private Lives of the Sultans in Istanbul*: a history of the harem of the rulers of the Ottoman empire from the fifteenth to twentieth centuries. This is a book without a thesis, designed simply to inform and entertain. Consider the beginning and end of the chapter on the sultan Süleyman the Magnificent:

> Süleyman was nearly twenty-six when he came to the throne. Foreign observers found him to be more pleasant than his grim father, and they were hopeful that his reign would bring better times, as Bartolomeo Contarini wrote before Süleyman's succession:
>
>> *He is twenty-five years of age, tall but wiry, and of a delicate complexion. His neck is a little too long, his face thin, and his nose aquiline. He has a shadow of a mustache and a small beard; nevertheless he has a pleasant mien, though his skin tends toward pallor. He is said to be a wise lord, and all men hope for good from his reign....*
>
> Süleyman was laid to rest in the beautiful *türbe* that Sinan had built for him behind the mosque, next to the tomb of his wife Roxelana, Selim's mother. A couplet from one of Süleyman's love poems to Roxelena comes to mind in the presence of their tombs, which stand side by side in the shade of the spectral cypresses, the Trees of Paradise
>
>> *All of a sudden, my glance fell upon her:*
>> *Like a cypress she was standing slender ...*[4]

Note the interest in Süleyman's physical appearance, not unlike a novel.

This end of the chapter is evocative, literally poetic, and, again, rather novelistic. It is not a conclusion of the kind one might find in a monograph or a scholarly article.

---

4 John Freely, *Inside the Seraglio: Private Lives of the Sultans in Istanbul* (Harmondsworth: Penguin Books, 2000), 50, 69.

Popular histories come in all kinds. Iris Chang's *The Rape of Nanking: The Forgotten Holocaust of World War II*[5] concerns massacres carried out by the Japanese army in the Chinese city of Nanking in 1937. Chang also aims at a popular audience. Her book, however, illustrates how popular histories can be an exception, or at least a partial exception, to how I have described them. The book does not have footnotes or endnotes but does use another form of citation: the back of the book lists all the sources used for page 49, then the sources used for page 50, and so on. This is a less convenient way to cite sources than footnotes or endnotes, but publishers think the general public is more willing to tolerate citations done in this way. The book also has a very general thesis, implied in part by the subtitle: Nanking experienced a holocaust and this event has been (largely) forgotten; as Chang herself notes, historians have established the basic outline of what happened at Nanking, and their estimates of noncombatant deaths over a few months in this one city range from 260,000 to 350,000. Her goal is to bring this event, ignored in general histories but known to scholars, to a broader public. The photographs included serve as further evidence for the atrocities discussed in the book – for example, a woman tied to a chair to be repeatedly attacked, Japanese soldiers smiling as a Chinese man is about to be beheaded. And Chang relies extensively on primary as well as secondary sources.

8.3 Online Secondary Sources

As noted in chapter 2.2, the bar for publishing online is low. Some websites post material that has already been published in book or journal form, using whatever quality controls those publishers have in place. Again, these tend, all other things being equal, to be strongest for university and commercial but academic presses. More often, however, websites are the first publishers of the material they contain. Again, as explained in 2.2, websites set up to make a profit – you can usually tell when they include advertisements – are especially prone to assemble material quickly from many contributors in order to procure lots of "clicks"; ensuring the quality of that material may be a lower priority. Such websites may not say who created the material, which can indicate a lack of accountability (for example, the commentary on the Declaration of Independence from Owlcation in chapter 2 is credited simply to "Jason"). Webpages affiliated with a college or university are comparatively likely to be created by people with expertise in the field, so looking for pages with ".edu" (or "ac.uk" in Britain) is a good idea; the same goes for government websites (so ".gov"). The websites of professional

---

5 London: Penguin Books, 1998.

associations dedicated to the study of history and historical museums can also often provide carefully chosen material (typically using a ".org" address). Bear in mind that, for instance, a blog post on such a site will still be more casual and more likely to represent "thoughts in progress" than, say, an article with citations.

Historians have to work for accuracy and to base their conclusions on carefully used evidence. Writers of monographs and scholarly articles tend to bear this especially in mind; there is an army of colleagues, mostly academics, whose job it is to find every flaw. For this reason, those authors tend to write in armor, bristling with footnotes, every tender spot as protected as possible, carefully explaining how the evidence leads to conclusions. Popular historians, by contrast, write to sell books. They, too, can labor to use evidence and use it well (Chang, for example). (When history professors, who presumably are well-informed about what they teach, assign popular histories, they choose the ones they think are well founded in the sources; they do the same when it comes to websites.) All historians make mistakes, and authors of monographs have been known to do worse and engage in outright fraud – although such cases are thankfully rare. But popular historians, being more lightly armored, move fast and so take less care to explain exactly how their sources support their conclusions. So do the authors of many websites. In all cases, *caveat lector*: reader beware.

PART IV: OTHER MATTERS

chapter nine

Counting: Primary Sources and Secondary Sources

Historians usually express themselves in words. But sometimes they make arguments using numbers. On occasion, you may need to know about things like standard deviations and P values; a basic course in statistics is never a bad thing. Most historians, however, use numbers with less sophistication. That does not mean, however, that numbers are a simple matter when it comes to history. Counting can be hard.

Take *cahiers de doléances*. The king of France had been forced to summon a traditional assembly, the Estates General, to meet in 1789 to deal with pressing problems of the realm; that meeting sparked the French Revolution. Each of the three legal estates in France – the clergy, the nobility, and everybody else – drew up complaints for the Estates General to consider. These collections of complaints were the *cahiers de doléances*. So the *cahiers de doléances* forwarded by the various estates from the various *bailliages*, or administrative districts, are excellent primary sources for what bothered people on the eve of the Revolution.

Why are these complaints important to historians? For one thing, some historians have long argued that the French Revolution was a response to long-standing complaints of the bourgeoisie or middle class – merchants, bankers, doctors, lawyers, and so on – about noble legal privileges, tax exemption for nobles, restrictions on commerce, and the monarchy's tight control over government and government policy. A second group of historians has argued that there was no real conflict between the bourgeoisie, on the one hand, and the nobility and the monarchy, on the other. The cahiers can help decide who is right here. Since the bourgeoisie dominated the third estate, its complaints were basically those of the bourgeoisie. The cahiers are a window that allows one to see how the bourgeoisie's concerns stacked up against those of the nobility.

But how to weigh the importance of this or that issue to the different estates? Here are a few of the concerns that appear in the cahiers that the first group of historians believe had a role in bringing on the Revolution:

- Fiscal equality: Some historians have argued that the bourgeoisie were very concerned about "fiscal equality" among the estates. Should the nobility and clergy lose their exemption from the chief taxes of the kingdom?
- Legal equality: A related issue was the legal inequality among the estates: should this be abolished?
- Control of taxation by the Estates General: should the Estates General, and not just the king, have a say in taxation, something it had not exercised in more than a century?
- Economic freedom in general: some in France were calling for economic deregulation, what might be called economic freedom.

It would be natural to turn to the cahiers simply to count up how many complaints or demands were made about these issues.

So now try to do that, just from one cahier. Here are portions of the cahier of the nobility sent in from the *bailliage* of Blois, in central France.[1] The comments will keep a running total of the issues listed above.

The object of every social institution is to confer the greatest possible happiness upon those who live under its laws.

Happiness ought not to be confined to a small number of men; it belongs to all. It is not an exclusive privilege to be contested for; it is a common right which must be preserved, which must be shared, and the public happiness is a source from which each has a place to draw his supply....

Art. 2. A tax is a partition of property.

This partition ought not to be otherwise than voluntary; in any other case the rights of property are violated: Hence it is the indefeasible and inalienable right of the nation to consent to its taxes.

According to this principle, which has been solemnly recognized by the king, no tax, real or personal, direct or indirect, not any contribution whatsoever, under whatsoever any name or form, may be established without the consent and free and voluntary approval of the nation. Nor may said power of consenting to a tax be

So does this mean the nobility of Blois are asking for equality before the law? Maybe; the matter is unclear. Perhaps this counts as 0 complaints/demands or as 1 complaint/demand? I will mark this ambiguity by counting it as 0 (if you think this complaint does not count) or as 1 (if you think this really is a call for legal equality). So, "0 or 1" or "0–1."

This is a pretty strong statement that the Estates General should have a role in taxation. Control of taxation to the Estates General: 1

---

1 "Typical Cahier of 1789," ed. University of Pennsylvania Department of History, *Translations and Reprints from the Original Sources of European History* 4, 5 (1898), 8–23.

transferred or delegated by the nation to any magistracy or any other body, or exercised by the provincial, city or communal assemblies: superior and inferior courts shall be especially charged to attend to the execution of this article, and to prosecute as exactors those who may undertake to levy a tax which has not received the proper sanction.

All public loans are, properly speaking, taxes in disguise, since the property of the kingdom is affected and hypothecated[2] for the payment of capital and interest. Therefore, no loan, under whatsoever form or denomination, may be effected without the consent of the nation assembled.

Again, a demand that the Estates General consent to taxation. How should one count this? Is it a second demand or simply an amplification of the previous paragraph? Control of taxation to the Estates General: 1 (if you do not think this is a second demand) or 2 (if you think it is).

Since the greater number of the taxes and imposts established up to this time have not yet received the sanction of the nation, the first business of the assembled estates will be to abolish all without exception; at the same time, in order to avoid the inconvenience resulting from an interruption in the payment of interest on the public debt and the expenses of government, the nation assembled, by virtue of the same authority, shall re-establish them, collecting them under a title of a free gift during the session of the Estates General and up to the time when they shall have established other taxes as may seem to them desirable.

This presents the same problem as the previous paragraph. Control of taxation to the Estates General: 1–3

A tax is no other thing than a voluntary sacrifice which each person makes of his particular property in favor of the public power, which protects and guarantees all. It is therefore evident that the tax ought to be proportioned to the interest which each has in preserving his property, and consequently the value of his property. In accordance with this principle the nobility of the *bailliage* of Blois believes itself duty bound to lay at the feet of the nation all the pecuniary exemptions which it has enjoyed or might have enjoyed up to the present time, and it offers to contribute to the public needs in proportion with other citizens, upon condition that the names of *taille*[3] and *corvée*[4] be suppressed and all direct taxes be comprised in a single land tax in money....

Here is a demand for fiscal equality, especially noteworthy coming from the nobility, who benefited from tax exemption. Fiscal equality: 1

[Various complaints and requests follow.]

The free and voluntary renunciation which the order of the nobility is about to make of its pecuniary privileges gives it the right to demand that no exemption whatsoever shall be retained in favor of any class of citizens. We have no doubt that the clergy will voluntarily consent to bear all taxes in common with citizens of other orders,[5] in proportion to their possessions; and we demand that the privileges

So, the discussion comes back to fiscal equality. Should this passage be counted as a second call for fiscal equality or just a drawing out of the implications of the call for fiscal equality listed previously? Can one argue that each group called upon to lose tax exemption (clergy, free cities, etc.) should count as one demand each? Perhaps, but I will not do so here for simplicity's sake. Fiscal equality: 1–2

---

2 I.e., pledged as security for debt.

3 The single largest tax in the country, from which the nobility and clergy were exempt.

4 A tax in the form of forced labor, from which the nobility and clergy were exempt.

5 That is, estates.

of free cities, of stage masters, of sealers of weights and measures and of all other persons to be abolished, in order that the tax shall affect all persons and places in proportion to the net product of their incomes. …

The principal assistance which agriculture awaits at this moment from the representatives of the nation is as follows:

1.   Absolute freedom in the sale and circulation of grain and produce;

2.   A regulation favoring the redemption of socome[6] and other burdensome taxes, the drainage of swamps, the division of communal lands;[7]

3.   Government encouragement in the production of better grades of wool and the breeding of cattle.…

The leading ideas [presented to us] … which we have determined to incorporate in our demands are the following: …

2.   That the law exempting from the payments of *taille* each rural inhabitant who has twelve children be re-enacted, and in case of the total suppression of the *taille* some equivalent compensation be made. …

7.   That any bill signed by a nobleman be declared a bill of honor.…[8]

10. That the law prohibiting all persons not noble from carrying arms be put in force, and that precautions be taken to assure its execution.…

Here is a call for economic deregulation. More economic freedom in general: 1

Hm … these demands seem to be for *economic regulation. What does one do with them? We had not gone into this source looking for demands against the proposals to be counted.*

Again, this appears to be a demand for government intervention in the economy.

Here is a request for a kind of fiscal inequality, albeit not one related to legal estates. What does one do with it?

A problem similar to the one noted previously, and indeed a clearer problem: these two demands are for legal inequality. Nobles are to have privileges that others will lack.

If you can see anything here, it's that counting complaints is more complicated than one might have expected. Sometimes it's not clear whether an item fits a category or not. Worse, sometimes it's unclear whether items should be counted as one item or two (or more). And it can become apparent that the items one planned to count are not all the pertinent items to the issue you are pursuing – consider, for example, those calls *for* fiscal inequality. There are a couple of lessons here. First, when working through a primary source to generate numbers, one will likely have to comb through the source twice. The first reading is reconnaissance, to get an idea of what there is to be counted and what problems counting might pose, and so be positioned to develop some rules or policies for how you will go about counting. The second time is for real, to actually count. (Of course, I am not recommending that you should comb through the source first so you can decide on what to count in order to bias your ultimate conclusion; that would be a very wrong

---

6 A lord's right to demand his peasant tenants have their grain ground only at the lord's mill – for a fee.

7 Land farmed in common by peasant villagers.

8 This restricted what court could hear in a dispute over a debt owed by a noble.

Table 9.1 Complaints in *cahiers de doléances*, 1789

Cahiers de doléances which supported:	of the nobility %	of the 3rd estate %
Equality before the law	23	17
Abolition of *lettres de cachet*	68.65	74
Abolition of interference in the judicial procedure by the government	47	40
Introduction of Habeas Corpus	40	31
Giving accused legal representation	24	35
Insistence on the establishment of a constitution as a precondition of any further grant of taxation	64	57
Division of legislative power between the king and the Estates General	52	36
Giving legislative power to the Estates General only	14	20
Regular meetings of the Estates General	90	84
Parliamentary immunity	24	16
Control of taxation to the Estates General	81	82
Fiscal equality	88	86
Ministerial responsibility to the Estates General	73	74
A constitutional regime in general	62	49
Liberty of the Press	88	74
Freedom of commerce	35	42
Abolition of monopolies	59	72
More economic freedom in General	45	66
Abolition of seigneurial rights	14	64

[30, 52]

thing to do.) Another lesson is that you may need to produce explanations of how you carried out the counting. How did you determine, for example, that there were two demands for fiscal equality (if that was your conclusion) rather than one? Essentially, you need to at least tell your reader your rules for counting. If you are very rigorous, and the items counted are not too many, you might have foot- or endnotes for specific instances.

A good historian figures out how to execute a count in a way that gets meaningful results but also avoids some of the problems this or that source presents when it comes to counting. Consider table 9.1, which counts concerns from many *cahiers de doléances*, put together by T.C.W. Blanning, based on numbers published by Guy Chaussinand-Nogaret, who himself relied on numbers produced by Sasha Weitman, who in turn used work by Beatrice Hyslop.

I will generally simply refer to Blanning or Chaussinand-Nogaret for convenience. The table's goal is to illuminate how concerned nobles were with various issues compared with the third estate (that is, everyone not considered nobility or clergy). I have put in **bold** the categories discussed previously.

Notice the difference between how Blanning counted these items and the way I tried to do so above. Instead of counting how many times an issue appears in the cahiers, Chaussinand-Nogaret looked at *how many cahiers* (comparing nobility and third estate) raise an issue. This allows him to avoid one of the difficulties we identified in the counting: whether a later instance of this or that issue should indeed be counted as a second instance (for example, the previous trouble in counting "Control of taxation to the Estates General"). Such difficulties fall away. Of course, this approach is made possible by the fact that the numbers in the table come from many cahiers, not just the one examined. And, also, of course, Blanning's table does not eliminate the kind of judgment calls discussed above as to what counts as an instance of what complaint, such as what to do about the somewhat ambiguous wording of the first passage I commented on above, that might be read as a call for legal equality. In fact, Chaussinand-Nogaret looked at numbers of certain complaints as well as numbers of cahiers with those complaints. Here Chaussinand-Nogaret discusses the method regarding the former: "For one category of grievance could be compressed. Supposing a bailliage called for the suppression of the *aides* (excise taxes) and then demanded in a whole series of complaints the abolition of each one by name, I only counted this as a single grievance."[9]

This discussion has implications for when you read numbers used in secondary sources. Here, too, readers need to read carefully, and as in any secondary source, consider how well the evidence produced – in this case, in the form of numbers – really supports the conclusion the historian draws. It can take a special effort to do this, in that many readers tend simply to assume that numbers indeed support whatever conclusion it is asserted they support. That is not a good approach.

Consider a passage that accompanies the table. Blanning has been discussing the thesis that the Revolution was caused by demands of the third estate, especially the middle class or bourgeoisie, for more "liberalism" – that is, limited government in general, especially limits on royal power, and general legal and fiscal equality – against a nobility and monarchy that did not want these things. All the issues in the table in one way or another pertain to this issue of liberalism. Here is what Blanning concludes from the numbers:

> Even more striking was the coincidence of the views of the nobility and the Third Estate on how France should be reformed. Taking a representative sample of liberal demands, Table 1 [i.e., table 9.1] shows that, if anything, the nobles were *more* liberal than their bourgeois colleagues. Certainly it is impossible to infer any confrontation between two diametrically opposed classes.[10]

---

9 G. Chaussinand-Nogaret, *The French Nobility in the Eighteenth Century* (Cambridge: Cambridge University Press, 1985), 148.

10 T.C.W. Blanning, *The French Revolution: Class War or Culture Clash?*, 2nd ed. (New York: St. Martin's Press, 1998), 45.

The numbers do generally show the nobility to have been more liberal than the third estate, with the exceptions of "Giving legislative power to the Estates General only" (where the numbers in both cases are pretty low) as well as "Control of taxation to the Estates General" and "Ministerial responsibility to the Estates General" (with a one-percentage-point difference, the nobility and third estate were really neck and neck on these two matters). All that is true, until one considers the last four issues (starting with "Freedom of commerce"), all arguably economic issues: here, there is pretty clearly a difference between the nobility and the third estate, and on these the third estate comes out more on the liberal side. So, the sentence "Taking a representative sample of liberal demands, [table 9.1] shows that, if anything, the nobles were *more* liberal than their bourgeois colleagues" is not entirely correct, unless one also argues that the issues listed before those last four were simply more important than those four – always a possibility. Blanning's next sentence, however, would still seem to hold: "Certainly it is impossible to infer any confrontation between two diametrically opposed classes." On the issues listed in table 9.1 as a whole, there was a lot of agreement between the nobility and the third estate. The moral of the story, as with everything else: read and think about numbers, including tables of numbers, carefully.

chapter ten

What Is in It for You?

In chapter 1, I suggested that discovering what happened in the past cannot in itself tell you how things should be in the present or future. A gap yawns between "was" (or "is") statements and "ought" statements. So, I do not think reading history can be expected to make you a more moral or ethical person. It will not enable you to tell right from wrong.

Perhaps, however, in a restricted sense, reading history can improve your character. The discussion in chapter 1 provides a starting point. I said that just because some people conclude whatever suits them from primary sources, you do not have to do likewise. "Some people," I said, "are more careful than others. Some people are more self-disciplined than others. Some people are more honest than others. It's better to be careful, disciplined, and honest."

Now, philosophers have long identified what they call "intellectual virtues." The term "virtue" should not mislead. These intellectual virtues are distinct from what are called "moral virtues," which have to do with ethical behavior, although certainly some virtues can be both moral and intellectual, depending on how they are exercised. "Intellectual virtues" are mental dispositions that help one reason one's way effectively to knowledge. Dispositions like, for example, carefulness, self-discipline, and honesty.[1] You should also note that intellectual virtues are not the same as raw intelligence. Very, very brainy people can be exceptionally unvirtuous when it comes to intellectual virtues.

These virtues are implied by some of the discussion in the other chapters in this book. Consider a modest example of self-discipline: I suggested in the previous chapters that

---

1 I should note that although I draw here on philosophers' discussions of intellectual virtues, my names for these virtues, or even the virtues themselves, are not always those identified by philosophers.

you will often, even generally, need to reread sources. It really would be less work to read them once and be done, but you should resist that temptation if you want to read well and reach sound conclusions. In other words, you need to exercise self-discipline. You also need to read with care, considering details and noting evidence that conflicts with other evidence you may have already found in the source. And you need to be honest. You might find some conclusions more attractive than others – it would be really great if prehistoric people were matriarchal, for example – but you need to be willing to acknowledge, to yourself and others, when the evidence goes against what you want to be true, or when the evidence simply does not support what you want to be true. Obviously, these intellectual virtues can be closely related, as the examples of carefulness and honesty show.

There are other intellectual virtues. Imagination enables one to come up with some of those alternative conclusions yourself – helpful in reading primary or secondary sources, especially argumentative ones like monographs and articles. It plays a role similar to that of inspiration, discussed in chapter 1, although inspiration is not itself a virtue. Open mindedness leads one to be willing to consider seriously conclusions different from, and even contradictory to, the ones that you have reached. Impartiality is obviously closely allied with open mindedness. I could go on.

There is a problem here. It is all well and good to say that these virtues are valuable to get knowledge, including historical knowledge. But "Be virtuous!" does not seem to be very helpful advice. How can you actually acquire these or any other intellectual virtues? And can reading history help?

Aristotle, who kicked off the tradition of reflecting on intellectual virtues, provided a clue as early as the fourth century BC. He argued that a virtue is a habit. A virtuous person is someone who routinely exercises virtue. Now, Aristotle had moral virtues in mind here; he thought that intellectual virtues come from education. But since his time, it has become apparent that a lot of reasoning is done without being very aware of the principles that reasoning uses. For example, people do not always think "I must be impartial" when they think impartially. Such principles – such virtues, one might say – are habitual. So intellectual virtues are cultivated by practicing them; they need to become habits, things one does without thinking about them. They need to become second nature.

And here is where reading history comes in. Reading history provides the reader with opportunities to exercise intellectual virtues and so to develop them; in other words, to develop good intellectual habits. The more you exercise those virtues, the better you can get at them, and in particular the more habitual they can become. And so reading history can, in that sense, make you virtuous. It can shape your character, at least in terms of intellectual virtues. If intellectual virtues are a matter of habit, you will see their impact not just when doing history, but in coming to conclusions from evidence in general, in gaining evidence-based knowledge generally.

But this proposal comes with a warning. Given what I have said, if anyone should be virtuous in an intellectual sense, it should be historians. Yet it is all too common to find historians exercising intellectual vices rather than virtues. One of the enemies of intellectual virtue is passion, which overwhelms the mind and directs the intellect in ways that are undisciplined, closed minded, and so on. Such passions might be about anything, such as whom to vote for or how much house to buy. Examples of historians overcome by such passion are not hard to find. Yes, passion can be intellectually useful. It can even inspire. But inspiration (such as the kind discussed in chapter 1) needs to be followed up with careful – and dispassionate – assessment of evidence, which is where the intellectual virtues come in.

So can reading history make you (intellectually) virtuous? I still want to suggest that it can – or at least, that it can help. My hope is that by being more self-conscious in developing intellectual virtues, in getting into the habit of exercising intellectual virtues, you are more likely to become intellectually virtuous. And reading history in the ways discussed in this book can help you do so. This may sound a bit like that unhelpful piece of advice, "Be virtuous!" But the idea is to exercise intellectual virtues not all in one go, but self-consciously and repetitively. Maybe, just maybe, you can in this way become (intellectually) virtuous step by step. That, too, is part of the promise of reading history.

Appendix: Questions and Tips

Collected here for convenience are questions and the occasional tip from this book's chapters.

Primary sources

First-order basic questions

Who, what, where, when? *Who produced the source? What kind of source is it? (E.g., a personal letter? A law?) When was it produced? Where was it produced?*

Audience? *Who seems to have been the expected audience?*

Literacy? *How literate was the society? What kinds of people were literate? What implications do your answers have for author and audience?*

Preservation? *How was the source preserved? Who would have preserved it and why?*

Meaning? *Is the source trying to say or show something? If so, in your own words, explain what that might be.*

Limits imposed by time and place? *Do your answers to the above set of questions – about who produced the source and so on – in any way influence or limit what conclusions you can draw?*

Second-order basic questions

Conclusions about time and place? *What conclusions can you draw from the source about the time and place that produced it?*

Actions? *Does the source provide evidence of actions taken by people in the past? If so, what conclusions can you draw from those actions? How well informed can you suppose the writer to have been about the events recounted? How reliable a reporter?*

Authority? *What or whom does the source seem to view as authoritative?*

Groups? *Does the source divide people into groups in any way? If so, what are those groups? Does the source make assumptions about how those groups, or members of them, do or should relate to one another? About how individuals relate to one another?*

Relationships? *What kinds of connections between people can you identify?* This may be another way of getting at the previous question.

Good and bad? *Does the source make moral distinctions? If so, what is viewed as good? As bad? What values does the source seem to assume?*

Assumptions? *What does the author assume to be normal and natural – or at least possible and calling for no special comment? (This question can be closely related to the previous one.)*

Argument? *If the source makes an argument, what is it? What issues seem to be debated in this society?*

Explain? *Does the source attempt to explain anything? If so, how does it go about doing so?*

Assumptions? *What knowledge or conditions does the source take for granted? This can serve as evidence of what was expected in the time and place that produced the source.*

Cause or effect? *Do your conclusions help you identify causes or effects of events or developments you have studied?*

Tip: **Try to read against the grain.**

Third-order basic questions

Representativeness? *How representative is the source?*

Larger questions? *Do your conclusions have implications for your understanding of larger questions historians have about the period you're studying?*

Continuity and change? *Do your conclusions imply change or continuity between the time that produced the source and earlier or later history?*

Relationship with the present? *Do your conclusions imply change or continuity between past and present?*

Tip: **Be prepared to reread the source.**

Some additional questions especially pertinent to certain kinds of primary sources:

Narrative sources, literary sources, and treatises

Reliability? *Could the reporter have been a bad reporter and so have gotten things wrong?*

Sources? *Where did the source get its information?*

Theme? *This is a version of asking about the source's* **meaning?** *Does the source repeat certain ideas to give them special prominence?*

And some prior questions that may particularly apply here:

Good and bad? *Does the source make moral distinctions? If so, what is viewed as good? As bad? What values does the source seem to assume?*

Assumptions? *What does the author assume to be normal and natural – or at least possible and calling for no special comment? (This question can be closely related to the previous one.)*

Tip: **For these sources in particular, do not forget to read against the grain!**

Material evidence

Art

Iconography? *Do elements of the work have iconographic significance; if so, what?*

Multiple cultures? *Does the work incorporate elements from more than one culture?*

Style? *Is the work's style or way of representing the world different from works of other periods or places?*

Archaeological evidence

What is the source made of?
What other evidence was found with the source?

Cognate sources and multiple sources

Agreement? *On what matters do they agree? Such agreement helps bolster their reliability, at least on those matters where they agree.*

Contradiction? *On what matters do the sources contradict each other? Such variance undermines their reliability, at least on those matters where they counter each other. Can you identify why one source might be more worthy of belief on such matters than the other?*

Compare and contrast? *What similarities and differences do you find between the two sources? How can similarities be used to highlight contrasts? What do the contrasts reveal about the contexts that produced the sources? (Or how can you explain the contrasts?)*

Secondary sources

Questions for monographs and articles

What is the topic?
What is the thesis?
How does the work respond to the historiography?
What is the overall argument in support of the thesis?
How strong is the evidence and the argument from that evidence?
Does the historian deal with evidence that undermines (or at least appears to undermine) the thesis? *If so, how well or badly?*
Does the work reflect the time in which it was written? *If so, does this introduce a bias? If so, does that bias undermine the argument?*
Tip: **Read the beginning and the end first. Then read the whole thing through. Likewise, read the beginning and end of each chapter before reading the chapter through.**

Tips for reading textbooks

As with a monograph, read the beginning and end of any chapter first. If the author makes larger points, they will likely appear there.

Pay attention to titles of chapters and subchapters.

First check the beginning and end of the chapter for any study questions. Such questions can be the author's way of directing you to especially important issues.

Pay special attention to pictures and even maps and their captions. While such material can be there just to make the book more fun, it can also be used to provide examples of statements in the text.

If the author provides a vocabulary list, pay attention to those terms in the text. The author thinks they are important.

Be prepared to read the text (at least) twice. Do so once before class; greater familiarity with the subject will probably help you follow what is going on in class. Read it again after class; in class, your instructor may highlight especially important issues, putting you in a better position to pick up on those matters when you reread the text.

Take notes as you go, either in the margin of the book or on a separate paper. You are much more likely to remember what you read if you do so. Highlighting with a marker or underlining is less likely to have this effect.

Suggestions for Further Reading

In addition to the various readings discussed in the text, as well as their references, here are a few suggestions to find out more. Some provide further food for thought on the subjects or issues raised; some appear because their bibliographies will lead the interested to further reading.

1 Introduction

A leading proponent of prehistoric matriarchy and goddess worship is Marija Gimbutas; see, for example, her "Symbols and Sacred Images of Old Europe," in *The Life of Symbols*, ed. Mary LeCron Foster and Lucy Jayne Botscharow (Boulder: Westview Press, 1990), 221–57. For criticism of the thesis of prehistoric matriarchy, see Margaret Beck, "Female Figurines in the European Upper Paleolithic: Politics and Bias in Archaeological Interpretation," in *Reading the Body: Representations and Remains in the Archaeological Record*, ed. Alison E. Rautman (Philadelphia: University of Pennsylvania Press, 2000), 202–14 and, wider ranging and more polemical, Cynthia Eller, *The Myth of Matriarchal Prehistory: Why an Invented Past Won't Give Women a Future* (Boston: Beacon Press, 2000). Alice B. Kehoe, "No Possible, Probable Shadow of Doubt," *Antiquity* 65, 246 (1991): 129–31, discusses the experiment with a string and the artifacts at Věstonice.

A superb account of the Reformation is Diarmaid MacCulloch's *The Reformation: A History* (New York: Penguin Books, 2003).

Several selections in *The Philosophy of History in Our Time*, ed. Hans Meyerhoff (Garden City, NY: Doubleday Anchor, 1959), deal with the problem of objectivity in history. (I have found the work excerpted there by Morton White particularly valuable.) Some of these issues are echoed in debates between postmodernists and their critics in *The Philosophy of History: Talks Given at the Institute of Historical Research, London, 2000-2006*, ed. Alexander Lyon Macfie (New York: Palgrave Macmillan, 2007).

Various books introduce readers to the primary sources for this or that time, place, or subject. For a number of these, see the series *The Routledge Guides to Using Historical Sources* (Routledge, 2008–). *The Middle Ages in Text and Texture: Reflections on Medieval Sources*, ed. Jason Glenn (Toronto: University of Toronto Press, 2011) offers scholars' riffs on particular sources from medieval Europe and how to read them.

2 From Manuscript to Edition

D.C. Greetham, *Textual Scholarship: An Introduction* (New York: Garland, 1994) covers various aspects of editing sources, including palaeography; Erick Kelemen, *Textual Editing and Criticism: An Introduction* (New York: W.W. Norton, 2009) centers on literature and a number of case studies but has a helpful bibliography.

Virginia Moore Carey, *Eastern Band Cherokee Women: Cultural Persistence in Their Letters and Speeches* (Knoxville: University of Tennessee Press, 2005) makes use, as the title implies, of letters by Cherokee women. For a wide-ranging and classic discussion relying on bishops' registers in thirteenth-century England, see Robert Brentano, *Two Churches: England and Italy in the Thirteenth Century* (Princeton: Princeton University Press, 1968), reprinted with an additional essay (Berkeley and Los Angeles: University of California Press, 1988).

M.I. Finley, *The World of Odysseus*, 3rd ed. (New York: Viking, 1977), reprinted with an essay by Bernard Knox (New York: NYRB Classics, 2002), is a classic that deals with, among other matters, the dating of Homeric epic.

3 Primary Source Basics and Two Documents of Practice

Naphtali Lewis's *Life in Egypt under Roman Rule* (Oxford: Oxford University Press, 1983), reprinted (Atlanta: American Society of Papyrologists, 1999), offers an accessible discussion with extended quotations from the papyri. Richard Alston, "Searching for the Romano-Egyptian Family," in *The Roman Family in the Empire: Rome, Italy, and Beyond*, ed. Michelle George (Oxford: Oxford University Press, 2005), 129–57, deals with the family discussed here.

For a wide-ranging discussion of occupied Japan that draws, from among many other sources, on letters written by Japanese citizens to General MacArthur, see John W. Dower, *Embracing Defeat: Japan in the Wake of World War II* (New York: W.W. Norton, 1999).

4 Narrative Sources and Cognate Sources

The definitive work on the Axe Man of New Orleans, drawing much on newspaper accounts, is Miriam C. Davis, *The Axeman of New Orleans: The True Story* (Chicago: Chicago Review Press, 2017). (I should disclose that I am married to the author.)

5 Literary Sources and Treatises

Recent English-language scholarship on the *Pañcatantra* is not common. Fortunately, there is McComas Taylor's *The Fall of the Indigo Jackal: The Discourse of Division and Pūrṇabhadra's Pañcatantra* (Albany: State University of New York Press, 2007), although not all of it will be for beginners. See also the introduction to *The Pañcatantra: The Book of India's Folk Wisdom*, trans. Patrick Olivelle (Oxford: Oxford University Press, 1997); Dany Poulose, "Gender Relations and Class Consciousness in the Pañcatantra," *Proceedings of the Indian History Congress* 75 (2014): 87–92.

For a wide-ranging point of entry to Christine de Pizan's works, see Nadia Margolis, *An Introduction to Christine de Pizan* (Gainesville, FL: University Press of Florida, 2011). Christine's political thought is also treated by Kate Langdon Forhan in *The Political Theory of Christine de Pizan* (Burlington, VT: Ashgate, 2002).

6 Material Evidence and Comparing Sources

Peter Adler and Nicholas Bernard's *ASAFO! African Flags of the Fante* (London: Thames and Hudson, 1992) offers an introduction to the subject, heavy on illustration. Silvia Forni and Doran H. Ross's *Art, Honor, and Ridicule: Fante Asafo Flags from Southern Ghana* (Toronto: Royal Ontario Museum and Fowler Museum at UCLA, 2017) is less introductory but has a helpful bibliography.

Simon Schama juxtaposes the paintings compared here in *Art and History: Images and Their Meaning*, ed. Robert I. Rotberg and Theodore K. Rabb (Cambridge: Cambridge University Press, 1988); I drew much from that discussion. That volume also provides other case studies of using art as a historical source. For more on Landseer's work, see Richard Ormond, *Sir Edwin Landseer*, with contributions by Joseph Rishel and Robin Hamlyn (New York: Rizzoli, 1981). Peter Burke discusses imagery and art associated with Louis XIV in *The Fabrication of Louis XIV* (New Haven: Yale University Press, 1992).

For the Baldock burial, see I.M. Stead and Valery Rigby, *Baldock: The Excavation of a Roman and Pre-Roman Settlement, 1968–72* (Gloucester: Alan Sutton Publishing, 1986). For larger issues, see Martin Millett, *The Romanization of Britain: An Essay in Archaeological Interpretation* (Cambridge: Cambridge University Press, 1990) and Keith J. Fitzpatrick-Matthews, "Subculture and Small Group Identity in Iron Age and Roman Baldock" in *Proceedings of the Sixteenth Annual Theoretical Roman Archaeology Conference, Cambridge 2006*, ed. B. Croxford, N. Ray, and N. White (Oxford: Oxbow Books, 2006), 150–71.

10 What Is in It for You?

The books on the philosophy of history suggested for chapter 1 pertain here too. I know of no work on intellectual virtues and history as a discipline specifically, but for intellectual virtues in general, see Robert C. Roberts and W. Jay Wood, *Intellectual Virtues: An Essay in Regulative Epistemology* (Oxford: Oxford University Press, 2007). A recent bibliography at the very least can be found in *Intellectual Virtues and Education: Essays in Applied Virtue Epistemology*, ed. Jason S. Baehr (New York: Routledge, 2016). A recent program for applied (or "regulative") epistemology that goes beyond intellectual virtues is Nathan Ballantyne, *Knowing Our Limits* (Oxford: Oxford University Press, 2019).

Index

Page references in *italics* indicate a figure; page references in **bold** indicate a table.